JERUSALEM PRAYER TEAM
"Pray for the Peace of Jerusalem..."

www.jerusalemprayerteam.org

DR. MICHAEL D. EVANS

OTHER RECENT NON-FICTION BOOKS
BY DR. MICHAEL D. EVANS

The Revolution

Cursed: The Conspiracy to Divide Jerusalem

Atomic Iran: Countdown to Armageddon

Jimmy Carter: The Liberal Left and World Chaos

Betrayed: The Conspiracy to Divide Jerusalem

*Showdown with Nuclear Iran: Radical Islam's Messianic
Mission to Destroy Israel and Cripple the United States*

*The Final Move Beyond Iraq:
The Final Solution While the World Sleeps*

*The American Prophecies:
Ancient Scriptures Reveal Our Nation's Future*

*Beyond Iraq: The Next Move
Ancient Prophecy and Modern Day Conspiracy Collide*

Why Christians Should Support Israel

Prayer of David

God Wrestling

The Unanswered Prayers of Jesus

I Shall Not Want

Living Fear Free

FICTION BOOKS

GameChanger

The Samson Option (GameChanger #2)

The Protocols

The Light

THE
FINAL
GENERATION

#1 *NEW YORK TIMES* BESTSELLING AUTHOR

MIKE EVANS

TimeWorthy
BOOKS

P.O. Box 30000, Phoenix, AZ 85046

Published by Time Worthy Books
P.O. Box 30000
Phoenix, AZ 85046

Library of Congress Cataloging-in-Publication Data
Evans, Michael

US	ISBN:	978-0-935199-36-9
Canada	ISBN:	978-0-935199-37-6
Hardcover	ISBN:	978-0-935199-38-3

Cover+Interior Design: Lookout Design, Inc.

Printed in the United States of America

19 18 17 16 15 14 13 12   2 3 4 5 6 7 8 9 10 11 12

While the troops of Mahomet II surrounded Constantinople in 1493 and it had to be decided if the Balkans would be under Christian or Mohammedan dominion for centuries, a local church council in the besieged city discussed the following problems: What color had the eyes of the Virgin Mary? What gender do the angels have? If a fly falls in sanctified water, is the fly sanctified or the water defiled?

It may be only a legend, as concerns those times, but peruse Church periodicals of today and you will find that questions just like this are discussed.

—RICHARD WURMBRAND

"For the coming of the Son of Man will be just like the days of Noah. For as in those days before the flood they were eating and drinking, marrying and giving in marriage, until the day that Noah entered the ark, and they did not understand until the flood came and took them all away; so will the coming of the Son of Man be. Then there will be two men in the field; one will be taken and one will be left. Two women will be grinding at the mill; one will be taken and one will be left.

"Therefore be on the alert, for you do not know which day your Lord is coming. But be sure of this, that if the head of the house had known at what time of the night the thief was coming, he would have been on the alert and would not have allowed his house to be broken into. For this reason you also must be ready; for the Son of Man is coming at an hour when you do not think He will."

—MATTHEW 24:37-44

INTRODUCTION

WHEN SIGNS ALIGN

The final move has begun. We are in the middle of a
world revolution managed by this dear [Twelfth Imam].
A great awakening is unfolding.
One can witness the hand of Imam in managing it.
—MAHMOUD AHMADINEJAD

In December of 2010 an unemployed college graduate was told he could not sell fruit on the streets of Tunis without a license. Desperate for work, the young man had become a street merchant to survive, and when even that was denied by the repressive Tunisian regime, he set fire to himself in protest. A few hours later he died as a result of the burns.

This extreme act of despair sent a ripple through the Tunisian population that was already wearied by massive unemployment and the draconian policies of their government. Social media sites such as Facebook and Twitter helped groups communicate their complaints and organize protests. Demonstrations across the country multiplied despite the ramifications: Roughly sixty people were killed as government troops tried to suppress the gatherings.

On January 14, 2011, thousands descended on the town center of Tunis, calling for President Zine al-Abidine Ben Ali to step down. A state of emergency was declared and a curfew leveled. Police attacked the mob with tear gas and batons and fired shots into the crowd, but protesters continued to pour into the streets, choking traffic to a standstill. Fearful of what would happen next, France and Germany urged tourists to leave the country as soon as possible and advised others to cancel any trips scheduled to Tunisia in the immediate future.

Unable to find a way to placate the populace and the mobs, early the next morning al-Abidine Ben Ali fled the country and announced he was stepping down from power. A new parliamentary election would take place as soon as possible.

The "Arab Awakening" had begun.

In the coming weeks you couldn't listen to the radio, turn on TV news, or pick up a newspaper and not see or hear about something happening in the Middle East. In subsequent weeks, President Mubarak stepped down in Egypt, civil war broke out in Libya, and untold hundreds were killed as the governments of Jordan, Bahrain, Syria, Yemen, and Iran violently suppressed all protests.

As the Egyptians cleaned the streets after Mubarak's downfall, Mahmoud Ahmadinejad addressed a gathering in Tehran's *Azadi* (Freedom) Square. They were celebrating the thirty-second anniversary of the Islamic Revolution of 1979. He welcomed the Egyptian uprising as a continuation of that revolution, declaring, "[The] Iranian nation is your friend, and it is your right to freely choose your path."[1] He also used the opportunity to declare his apocalyptic visions, pledging to help replace capitalism and democracy with a new Islamic world order:

> *The final move has begun. We are in the middle of a world revolution managed by this dear [Twelfth Imam]. A great awakening is unfolding. One can witness the hand of Imam [Mahdi] in managing it.*[2]

In recent months Ahmadinejad has been priming the pump for this new world order, appearing before the U.N. General Assembly in September of 2010—just days after the anniversary of the September 11 attacks. He opened his speech by calling for the coming of the Shia messiah to appear: "Oh God, hasten the arrival of Imam Al-Mahdi and grant him good health and victory and make us his followers and those who attest to his rightfulness." He followed this with accusations that the United States had planned and orchestrated the attacks of 9/11 in an attempt to reverse U.S. economic decline and as an excuse to invade countries in the Middle and Near East. He outlined his hopes to see the Islamic-dominated United Nations General Assembly wrest control of the body from the veto power of the Security Council nations. He also stated, "I would like to here propose that the year 2011 be proclaimed the year of nuclear disarmament and 'Nuclear Energy for All, Nuclear Weapons for None,'" in further attempts to cloak Iran's nuclear ambitions.

On June 15, 2011, he addressed the Shanghai Cooperation Organization (SCO)—a security group regarded as a NATO rival that is led by China and Russia. Iran is an observer nation in the SCO and has requested permission to join the group as a member state. Ahmadinejad told the body, "I believe together we can reform the way the world is managed. We can restore the tranquility of the world."[3] Only a few days later he stated, "If we want to make a bomb, we are not afraid of anyone, and we are not afraid to announce it. No one can do a damn thing."[4]

Since becoming the Iranian president in August 2005, Mahmoud Ahmadinejad has seldom minced words about the world he hopes to create—a world without the Great Satan of the United States at its head, and one in which the Little Satan of Israel is "wiped off the face of the Earth." He longs for a world in which the Twelfth Imam, a Shia Islamist messiah figure also known as the Mahdi, establishes a supreme Caliphate in Iraq, from which he will rule the world.[5] This might all be saber rattling and Islamist propaganda if it weren't that Ahmadinejad's vision of the end of the age is almost a mirror opposite of what Jesus said would happen just as the events of the book of Revelation were heating up.

ARE THE PROPHETIC PIECES NEARLY IN PLACE?

A diabolical counterfeit of God's ultimate plan of salvation seems to be spreading across the Middle East—and is playing out just as foretold in the Bible. While Western Christians seem to be growing more complacent and concerned with their personal comfort and success, a prophetic storm is gathering in the Middle East. Radical Islamists are preparing for the final battle, believing it will usher in a new age of Islamist supremacy. Do you find these events as chilling as I do?

I have been a Middle East correspondent for more than three decades and an advisor on the Middle East for just as long. In that time I have written almost two-dozen books on the Middle East and radical Islam, many of them discussing their relationship to the events of the book of Revelation. I have studied the prophecies about the end of the age given by Jesus, the Old Testament prophets, and the New Testament apostles. I have read and reread books on Bible eschatology written by experts, teachers, and scholars. And in all my research and years of experience, there has been no other time when the signs of Jesus' imminent return were happening with the intensity we are seeing today. Bible prophecy after Bible prophecy points to the likelihood that the last generation before Jesus' return is now on the Earth, and the last lap for the Church has begun.

I know many wise men and women will take this declaration with at least a grain of salt. In fact, someone declared that Jesus would return on May 21, 2011, only to be proven spectacularly wrong. He was ridiculed by both believers and non-believers. At the same time, popular Christian leaders are suggesting that the book of Revelation actually has more to do with the Romans of John's time than as a prognosis for what will happen at the end of the age, throwing many into confusion. Others have touted that no one is going to be "left behind" in the Rapture. All will be saved in the end, despite what Scripture says. It is eerily reminiscent of the days before the flood, as Noah called on humanity to repent. They ridiculed and scoffed, only to realize too late that Noah had had their best interests at heart.

Personally, I have neither the desire to be a prophet of doom nor someone crying "wolf" about something that is still in the future. However, when I see the handwriting on the wall, I feel the obligation to speak up. Neither am I here to tell you to ready your bomb shelter, but I am here to say you may need to change your thinking.

The early church called the message of Jesus' soon return "The Blessed Hope." They saw it as a message of liberation that gave them the resolve to live righteously before their God. That is the message I want you to get from reading this book. When you put it down, I don't want you to be filled with dread; I want you to be excited about what God is doing to seek and save the lost. I also want you to be more determined that as few as possible will be left on Earth the day Jesus calls us home.

In order to understand that message, we must first understand the gravity of where we are on God's timeline. Time is of the essence. There is no more room for the "business as usual, let me work out my own personal salvation" complacency that grips our culture, our marketplaces, our political arenas, and—unfortunately—far too many of our churches today. Our own personal pursuits of life, liberty, and happiness will not get us through the twenty-first century as they did in the last half of the twentieth.

The American dream is turning into a nightmare right before our eyes, blinding many to the converging prophetic storms gathering before us. People, including many Christians, have grown dull of hearing. As Solomon warned us in Proverbs, now more than ever, *"the complacency of fools shall destroy them"* (Proverbs 1:32).

Jesus said that the final days before His return would be like those of Noah before the flood. Humanity would be obsessed with the issues of prosperity, entertainment, and self-fulfillment: *"eating and drinking, marrying and giving in marriage"* (Matthew 24:38). In Luke, Jesus expanded further on this saying:

> *"It was the same as happened in the days of Lot: they were eating, they were drinking, they were buying, they were selling, they were planting, they were building; but on the day that Lot went out from Sodom it rained fire and brimstone from heaven and destroyed them all. It will be just the same on the day that the Son of Man is revealed.*
>
> *Remember Lot's wife. Whoever seeks to keep his life will lose it, and whoever loses his life will preserve it."*
> —Luke 17:28-30, 32-33

We must wake up to the realization that the Bible prophecies of Daniel, Ezekiel, and Revelation are quickly moving into position for God's final checkmate of Satan. Israel is likely within a decade or less of facing the greatest threat to its existence: the development of an Iranian nuclear bomb. Not only that, but the framework for a one-world government and common world currency is already in the minds of many—just as Ahmadinejad outlined before the United Nations last fall, to the accolades of most of the delegates in the General Assembly. A perfect storm of religious extremism and those who would profit from it is gathering to oppose Judaism, Christianity, and Western Secularism alike, while the U.S. and the E.U. take the course of appeasement.

The more I study these things, the more I see we are in a critical place for action on God's prophetic timeline. While some may choose to ignore where we are, none of us should be caught by surprise. Certainly others over the centuries since Jesus ascended have looked at these signs and said that Jesus' return was near, only to be proven wrong. However, in those days they highlighted, at most, a handful of prophecies at once. Today we are seeing *all* of the signs happening—moving into alignment, if you will—and *all* of them happening with increasing intensity. Even if we don't know the exact moment or day Jesus will return, we need to realize we are in the midst of the *season* of His return. Moreover, we must heed His instructions that it is not a season for hiding but for action.

Certainly wise men and women have been looking for the Second Coming of Jesus Christ since the ink was still wet on the parchment of the book of Acts, but until now, few of the necessary prerequisites have been in place. As the voices of those pointing to the signs of the end of the age rise to a crescendo, we must remember the promise:

> **Surely the Lord God does nothing**
> **Unless He reveals His secret counsel**
> **To His servants the prophets. —Amos 3:7**

We must understand our time in the context of biblical prophecy.

Other generations have read the Scriptures and realized they lived in a prophetic time. We need to do the same. God has incredible things for us to do before we are taken away. While some look at these future events as the greatest time of catastrophe the world has ever experienced, it will also be the greatest time of God's intervention on behalf of those who call on His name. But there is much to do before He comes!

And it is time to begin.

PART ONE:

SEVEN MINUTES
TO MIDNIGHT

"Now learn the parable from the fig tree:
when its branch has already become tender and puts forth its leaves, you know
that summer is near; so, you too, when
you see all these things, recognize that
He is near, right at the door. Truly I say
to you, this generation will not pass away
until all these things take place."

—MATTHEW 24:32-34

CHAPTER ONE

A BRIEF, PROPHETIC HISTORY OF TIME

"How long will it be until the end of these wonders?" . . .
"My lord, what will be the outcome of these events?"

—DANIEL 12:6, 8

It's a view I have seen at least a half-dozen times, but it never fails to take my breath away. Stretched out before me is what the prophet Joel called *"the valley of Jehoshaphat"* (Joel 3:2). A few miles to the north of the hilltop where I stand, I can see the white-walled buildings of Nazareth glistening in the midday sun. Farther on and a bit to the east, I can see a shimmer that is the Sea of Galilee. Just to the north of that is the Golan Heights, one of the most strategically important mountain ranges in Israel. About eighteen miles to the northwest is the port city of Haifa on the Mediterranean Sea.

The Valley of Megiddo is tranquil and serenely beautiful with its patchwork of farms, roads, and small villages. As I look over it, I wonder how much longer it will remain that way. This is the very valley the Bible tells us will one day run with rivers of blood—the valley of the last battle before Jesus' return—the world-shattering Battle of Armageddon.

Looking over this expanse makes me wonder what it might be like to survey the history of prophecy in the same way I look over this valley. In my mind's eye I envision all the events of the Bible laid out before me like a great mountain range, both the historic and the prophetic, from the creation of the Earth to the day of Jesus' return. No one would be surprised to see that the highest peak was the resurrection of mankind's Messiah, Jesus. However, what might surprise many is that there is another peak, less known but almost as high, that happened just a handful of centuries before that. It was a pivotal time on the Earth that corresponded with some very important events: 1) the defeat of the Babylonian Empire, 2) the birth of the Persian Empire, and 3) the return of the Jews to Jerusalem to rebuild the Temple where Jesus would one day teach.

The ascents to these peaks were journeys of triumph and failure. They were marked by the fall from grace of Adam and Eve, which utterly thwarted God's original plan for humanity to live in Eden; nevertheless, these ascents were also fulfilled by men of great faith like Job and Abraham. Through Abraham, God was able to reconnect with humanity and initiate His plan for redemption through his descendants, the nation of Israel. There were peaks and valleys from there as well: failure under judges such as Jair, Jephthah, and Eli to live before God as His people; but dramatic revivals and victories under Gideon and Samson.

Israelites eventually grew weary of living under the authority of the prophets and demanded a king to make them like other nations, so God gave them Saul. However, Saul's fear of men overpowered his allegiance to God, and he led Israel into a dark place. Despite King Saul's failures, however, Israel flourished under King David and rose to become the greatest nation on the Earth under King Solomon. Then Solomon's son allowed the nation to divide into two kingdoms, the Northern Kingdom of Israel and the Southern Kingdom of Judah. Thereafter, the Jewish people had a long line of unrighteous kings that led to its ultimate capture and exile from the Land for seventy years.

It is at this point in prophetic history—when Israel failed as an independent nation, was taken captive, and looked as if it would pass into obscurity—that God intervened with His promises for the ultimate salvation of humanity, a plan that could not be thwarted by human frailties. He laid out His timeline for the coming of the Messiah and what would happen during the last days of the Earth.

To understand the framework of this prophetic plan—a plan that essentially spans the history of time—we need to go back and see what God told the prophets of this period, specifically Jeremiah, Daniel, and Ezekiel. It is only with a view from this peak of Bible prophecy that we can clearly see God's ultimate plan of redemption for Israel as a nation, which is also foretold in the book of Revelation.

THE CONTINENTAL DIVIDE OF PROPHECY

Sometime during Judah's exile in Babylon (around 538 BC), an old Jewish bureaucrat finished his daily devotional and rolled up his scroll of the writings of Jeremiah. Among the scriptures he read was Jeremiah 25:11-12:

> *This whole land shall become a ruin and a waste, and these nations shall serve the king of Babylon seventy years. Then after seventy years are completed, I will punish the king of Babylon and that nation, the land of the Chaldeans, for their iniquity.*

Seventy years. Curious. Sitting at his study table, he looked through his journals and writings. He calculated how long it had been since he was taken captive as a boy and brought to the city of Babylon. He sighed. According to all he had just read, Judah's seventy years of exile must be nearing its end. (See Daniel 9:1-3.) He realized he was living in a prophetic time.

Of course, this man was Daniel, who was captured as a youth, brought to Babylon to serve King Nebuchadnezzar, and then rose in authority as a Babylonian official. As Daniel read Jeremiah's prophecy, he knew that the time of Babylon's punishment had begun, just as Jeremiah had foreseen. Nebuchadnezzar's line had been dethroned, as his descendant Belshazzar had been "*weighed in the balances and found wanting*" (Daniel 5:27) and his kingdom "*divided and given to the Medes and Persians*" (Daniel 5:28). This had occurred the very night Daniel had read the handwriting on the wall. Darius the Mede now ruled as an appointed governor of Cyrus the Great, the first Persian emperor.

As Daniel sat pondering these things, he remembered two visions God had given him foretelling these events. The first, found in Daniel, chapter 2, was of a statue whose head was gold (representing Babylon), whose arms and torso were silver (representing the Medo-Persian Empire he was currently experiencing), whose stomach and thighs were bronze (the coming Greek civilization), whose legs were iron (the future Roman Empire), and whose feet were a mixture of iron and clay (a coalition of nations that would arise from the remnants of the Western and Eastern Roman Empires centuries later). Daniel knew that Persia had replaced Nebuchadnezzar's Babylon and was the second of the five kingdoms that would rule the Middle East in the years to come.

In the second vision, Daniel had been shown the succession of governments in the Middle East again. (See Daniel 7 and 8.) Now, knowing that Jeremiah's prophecy of Babylon's fall already had been fulfilled before his very eyes, Daniel realized it was time for Judah's exile to come to an end—and for the city of Jerusalem to be rebuilt. The transfer of power from Babylon to Persia had happened, yet the other half of the prophecy—the rebuilding of Jerusalem and the return of the Jews to the Promised Land—was yet to take place. Daniel wanted to know why. To find out, he began to pray and intercede for his nation, asking that no sin of the past would trip them up on their way out of exile:

"Alas, O Lord, the great and awesome God, who keeps His covenant and lovingkindness for those who love Him and keep His commandments, we have sinned, committed iniquity, acted wickedly and rebelled, even turning aside from Your commandments and ordinances. Moreover, we have not listened to Your servants the prophets, who spoke in Your name to our kings, our princes, our fathers and all the people of the land.

"O Lord, in accordance with all Your righteous acts, let now Your anger and Your wrath turn away from Your city Jerusalem, Your holy mountain . . . For Your sake, O Lord, let Your face shine on Your desolate sanctuary.

O Lord, hear! O Lord, forgive! O Lord, listen and take action! For Your own sake, O my God, do not delay, because Your city and Your people are called by Your name."—Daniel 9:4-6, 16-17, 19

In response, God sent the angel Gabriel to Daniel to outline His timetable for the future spiritual redemption of His Jewish people and all humanity, a redemption that would come through the Jewish Messiah. Then Gabriel went on to relate what will happen to the nation of Israel in the very last days. This entire timetable is laid out in Daniel 9:24-27, perhaps the most succinct and significant passage of prophecy in the entire Bible.

"Seventy weeks have been decreed for your people and your holy city, to finish the transgression, to make an end of sin, to make atonement for iniquity, to bring in everlasting righteousness, to seal up vision and prophecy and to anoint the most holy place. So you are to know and discern that from the issuing of a decree to

restore and rebuild Jerusalem until Messiah the Prince there will be seven weeks and sixty-two weeks; it will be built again, with plaza and moat, even in times of distress. Then after the sixty-two weeks the Messiah will be cut off and have nothing, and the people of the prince who is to come will destroy the city and the sanctuary. And its end will come with a flood; even to the end there will be war; desolations are determined. And he will make a firm covenant with the many for one week, but in the middle of the week he will put a stop to sacrifice and grain offering; and on the wing of abominations will come one who makes desolate, even until a complete destruction, one that is decreed, is poured out on the one who makes desolate."

In his commentary on the book of Daniel, James E. Smith calls this passage "the continental divide of biblical prophecy."[6] That makes sense. All prior events in biblical history lead to this point—what is now known as "Daniel's Seventy Weeks." From this point forward, though the road would be arduous, all events would lead to the Jews' spiritual redemption, offered by their "*Messiah the Prince.*" Then, abruptly, Gabriel says that "*the Messiah will be cut off and have nothing.*" This, of course, refers to the crucifixion of Jesus of Nazareth. However, you will notice Gabriel makes no mention of Jesus' resurrection or ascension, or the birth of the Church, which are monumental, historical events.

Gabriel makes no mention of these important events because there is a gap between the time the Jewish Messiah is "cut off" and Daniel's Seventieth Week. This gap would be the Church Age. Through the Messiah's sacrificial death and resurrection, spiritual salvation would come first to the Jews and then to the Gentiles, but throughout the Church Age God will deal primarily with Gentiles. All humanity would be offered reconciliation to God and freedom from sin through Jesus' blood. Those who chose to accept Him as their Savior and Lord would be forgiven and cleansed of all unrighteousness. Thus, they would live in God's spiritual kingdom on the Earth and go to Heaven when they died.

The Church Age was a mystery[7]—not revealed in Daniel's visions nor in Gabriel's message. All Daniel and the Old Testament believers knew was that at the end of seven and sixty-two weeks (or the end of the sixty-ninth week), their Prince, the Messiah, would be cut off and *eventually* another "prince who is to come" would make their Land desolate. The gap they did not see, because God kept it a mystery, was the Church Age. This would be a time when believers of all nations would take the message of Jesus the Messiah to the world.

At the end of the Church Age, the Seventieth Week would begin, when God would focus one last time on His Jewish people for a period of seven years.. At the end of that time, Jesus the Messiah would return to reign on Earth for a thousand years.

Daniel's Seventy Weeks are the prophetic backbone of the history of both the Jewish nation and all mankind, spanning the time from the rebuilding of Jerusalem (Daniel 9:25) until the defeat of the *"one who makes desolate"* (Daniel 9:27), so we need to take a closer look at them.

UNDERSTANDING THE SEVENTY WEEKS

During his visitation, the angel Gabriel tells Daniel:

> *"Seventy weeks have been decreed for your people and your holy city, to finish the transgression, to make an end of sin, to make atonement for iniquity, to bring in everlasting righteousness, to seal up vision and prophecy and to anoint the most holy place." —Daniel 9:24*

It is important to know that this prophecy was spoken to the Jewish people, not the Church that was to come. It explained how salvation would come to them through Jesus the Messiah—and then through them to all the Earth. It was to be the period in which God would:

» put a finish to transgression,

» make an end of sin,

» make atonement for iniquity,

» bring in everlasting righteousness,

» seal up (fulfill) vision and prophecy, and

» *anoint the most holy place.*

The coming of Jesus Christ and His crucifixion and resurrection were part of this plan, as are His Second Coming, His millennial reign, the completion of all visions and prophecy (see 1 Corinthians 13:8-12), and the coming of the New Jerusalem and the Fourth Temple (see Revelation 21:2-4).

The Messiah would first come to provide a way for human beings to be reconciled to God and escape the ultimate consequences of sin. It would be the age of those "called out"[8] from the ways of the world, those in His universal Church, to whom He would give authority and power to establish the kingdom of God on the Earth. When would this Messiah come? Again, Gabriel gave Daniel a specific timeline, just as God had given the Israelites a specific time of seventy years in Babylonian exile.

> *"So you are to know and discern that from the issuing of a decree to restore and rebuild Jerusalem until Messiah the Prince there will be seven weeks and sixty-two weeks; it will be built again, with plaza and moat, even in times of distress. Then after the sixty-two weeks the Messiah will be cut off and have nothing." —Daniel 9:25-26*

The "weeks" mentioned here are not seven-day periods but seven-year periods—weeks of years, if you will. Using these "weeks of years," there were three periods within Daniel's Seventy Weeks in which God would act for the final salvation of the Hebrew people:

» seven weeks from the decree to rebuild Jerusalem until it was finished,

» sixty-two weeks from the finishing of Jerusalem until the Messiah entered the city, and

» a final week that would take place after a period in which Jerusalem and the Temple were destroyed.

A countdown to the appearance and crucifixion of the Messiah would begin when a decree went out from the Persian king that the Jews had permission to rebuild the walls, plazas, moats, and streets of Jerusalem. That would take seven weeks, or 49 years. Then, from the rebuilding of Jerusalem until the coming of the Messiah, there would be sixty-two weeks (434 years). This would total sixty-nine weeks in all, or 483 years.

In the decades following Daniel's revelation, there were three decrees concerning the Jews made by Persian rulers:

1. In roughly 538 BC (the same year Daniel recorded this prayer and vision in Daniel 9), Cyrus the Great decreed that the Temple could be rebuilt and worship could return to Jerusalem. (See 2 Chronicles 36:22; Ezra 1:2-4; and Isaiah 44:28.)

2. Around 457 BC, Artaxerxes I proclaimed that all Ezra needed to reestablish worship and society in Jerusalem should be given to him out of the Persian treasuries. A contingent of Jews would

also be allowed to return to Jerusalem with
Ezra to finish the Temple's rebuilding. (See Ezra
7:12-24.)

3. *In the spring of 445 BC, in the twentieth year of
his reign, Artaxerxes I declared that Nehemiah
could return to Jerusalem to rebuild its gates
and walls. (See Nehemiah 2:6-8.)*

This last decree—the only one mentioning the rebuilding of
Jerusalem itself—was the one that began the countdown to the coming
of the Messiah. Thus, Daniel's Seventy Weeks began in the Jewish month
of Nissan, circa 445 BC.

Scholars do not recognize a specific historical event that marks the
end of the first period of forty-nine years. Some say it was when the walls
and streets of Jerusalem were finally complete; others mark it as the end
of the prophetic age for Judah and Israel. However, there is no significant
event in history distinctly tied to the end of this period.

We do know that the final book of the Old Testament, Malachi,
was written sometime during these forty-nine years (sometime between
430 BC and 398 BC, the latter date being forty-nine Jewish years after
Artaxerxes' second decree), and the reconstruction of Jerusalem's walls
and streets must have been completed sometime during the period as
well. However, what has stunned Bible scholars is that if you take the
forty-nine years and the next period of sixty-two weeks together, you
come to a startlingly important event.

In his 1882 book, *The Coming Prince*[9] (named after "*the prince who
is to come*" of the last part of Daniel 9:26, the person called the Antichrist
in the New Testament), Sir Robert Anderson did a critical study of
Daniel's vision of the Seventy Weeks. Looking back through historical
chronology, he determined that the first day of Nissan 445 BC would have
been March 14 when transposed onto the Gregorian calendar.

You should know that the Jews of the Old Testament did not measure years by the rotation of the Earth around the sun (365.25 days) as our modern calendars do (since the time of Pope Gregory XIII), but by the rotations of the moon around the Earth. Thus, the Jewish year during the time of Daniel measured only 360 days.

Using this Jewish calendar, Anderson determined the number of days in sixty-nine weeks of Jewish years (69 weeks x 7 years = 483 Jewish years, and then 483 x 360 days = 173,880 days). Anderson counted forward 173,880 days from March 14, 445 BC. According to his calculations, Daniel's sixty-nine weeks ended on April 6, 32 AD, the Sunday before Passover of that year, according to historical records; or, as he wrote in the preface to the tenth edition of his book,

> *That day, on which the sixty-nine weeks ended, was the fateful day on which the Lord Jesus rode into Jerusalem in fulfillment of the prophecy of Zechariah 9:9; when, for the first and only occasion in all His earthly sojourn, He was acclaimed as "Messiah the Prince, the King, the Son of David."*[10]

This, of course, describes what Christians today call Palm Sunday. Although being this exact with the dates so far back in history is difficult, Robert Anderson's analysis is still being echoed by Bible scholars today. It is the most remarkable example of the pinpoint accuracy of Bible prophecy ever recorded.

If you look more deeply into this passage in Daniel 9, you will see that at the end of the sixty-nine weeks, there would be an age that happened before the final week took place. The countdown on God's prophetic clock would pause with seven years left—or you could say it froze at seven minutes to midnight. It has been there ever since. During that gap:

> *"The people of the prince who is to come will destroy*

the city and the sanctuary."—*Daniel 9:26*

According to Scripture, during the interlude between the end of the sixty-ninth week and the beginning of the seventieth, Jerusalem and the Temple would again be destroyed. This happened in 70 AD when Titus decimated Jerusalem. Furthermore, the people of Israel would be scattered to the four corners of the Earth, which happened in 135 AD, when the Romans finally expelled all Jews from Jerusalem and Judea after the Bar Kokhba revolt. Rome was, of course, the fourth kingdom Daniel was shown in the vision God gave him, a vision that was the interpretation of King Nebuchadnezzar's dream of the statue. (Again, see Daniel 2.)

Scholars agree that "*the prince who is to come*" is the Antichrist— the ultimate manifestation of the spirit that has influenced rulers and kingdoms throughout history to persecute the people of God whenever and wherever they could. The people of "*the prince who is to come*" would not need to be people who served the Antichrist himself but those who bowed their knee to the spirit of antichrist at any time in history. We see this spirit in the Romans who destroyed Jerusalem, in the Nazis, in communists, and in religious and secular groups and governments throughout the Church Age. However, the final manifestation of this spirit, in the person of the Antichrist, will not take place until the dawn of Daniel's Seventieth Week.

Gabriel then sums up the period between "Messiah being cut off" and the end of the last week—the period we know as the Age of the Church—in one brief statement:

> "*And its end will come with a flood; even to the end there will be war; desolations are determined.*"—*Daniel 9:26*

In other words, during the time between Jesus' crucifixion and the beginning of Daniel's last week, there will be war continually somewhere on the planet. As the return of the Messiah nears, this will increase until it is not only constant but also widespread. Not only will war increase, but also human and natural "desolations"—what Jesus pointed to in foreseeing *"there will be great earthquakes, and in various places plagues and famines; and there will be terrors and great signs from heaven"* (Luke 21:11)—will increase. These things will build until the age's *"end will come like a flood."* Some people will see it coming, but as in the days of Noah, many will be caught unprepared because they chose to ignore the signs.

The rising of these apocalyptic waters will continue until the Antichrist finally appears to sign a peace accord with Israel and establish a brief time of security and détente upon the Earth. The signing of this ceasefire is the event Daniel was told would begin the Seventieth Week, one eschatological scholars call "The Tribulation." The Tribulation will be split into two, three-and-a-half-year periods by the Abomination of Desolation that is spoken of in various scriptures. As the angel Gabriel described it:

> *"And he* [the prince who is to come] *will make a firm covenant with the many* [Israel and other nations] *for one week, but in the middle of the week he will put a stop to sacrifice and grain offering; and on the wing of abominations will come one who makes desolate* [the Abomination of Desolation], *even until a complete destruction, one that is decreed, is poured out on the one who makes desolate." —Daniel 9:27* [inserts added]

After the Abomination of Desolation, the world will erupt in war again—a world war unequaled in history. The wrath of God will be poured out on the Earth to show the wages of sin in the hope that many will call upon the name of the Lord to be saved. *"The prince who is to come"*—the Antichrist—will call for Jewish genocide and systematically persecute any who do not bear a mark of allegiance to him.

The second half of Daniel's last week—what Jesus called the "*Great Tribulation*" (Matthew 24:21)—will see two-thirds of the world population killed in battles, plagues, and natural disasters, and it will culminate in the nations of the Earth coming to fight one last battle in the Valley of Armageddon. (For an outline of these events, see Appendix A: A Timetable of Prophetic Events.)

Without Jesus coming back to put an end to this period, the entire Earth would be destroyed. His return will usher in the Millennium, a time of peace and prosperity for all spoken of by the ancient prophets:

> *It will come about in the last days That the mountain of the house of the LORD Will be established as the chief of the mountains. It will be raised above the hills, And the peoples will stream to it.*
>
> *Many nations will come and say, "Come and let us go up to the mountain of the LORD And to the house of the God of Jacob, That He may teach us about His ways And that we may walk in His paths." For from Zion will go forth the law, Even the word of the LORD from Jerusalem.*
>
> *And He will judge between many peoples And render decisions for mighty, distant nations. Then they will hammer their swords into plowshares And their spears into pruning hooks; Nation will not lift up sword against nation, And never again will they train for war. —Micah 4:1-3*

And

> *And He will judge between the nations, And will render decisions for many peoples; And they will hammer their swords into plowshares and their spears into pruning hooks. Nation will not lift up sword against nation,*

And never again will they learn war. —Isaiah 2:4

The indefinite period between when the Messiah is *"cut off"* and when *"the prince who is to come"* establishes a peace accord with Israel would be the age of the Church. Jesus delineated this age in Matthew 28:19-20—a time when His authority would rest on His followers to:

> *"Go . . . and make disciples of all the nations, baptizing them in the name of the Father and the Son and the Holy Spirit, teaching them to observe all that I commanded you; and lo, I am with you always, even to the end of the age."* (Emphasis added.)

This age is a time dedicated to the salvation of Jews and Gentiles alike through the preaching of the Gospel of Jesus Christ and the work of every member of the Church. It will last as long as the Church is on the Earth, ending the day the trumpet sounds and those who belong to Jesus are taken in the Rapture. (See 1 Thessalonians 4:16-17; 1 Corinthians 15:50-58; Matthew 24:40-41.)

HOW CAN ISRAEL CUT A COVENANT IF THERE IS NO ISRAEL?

For much of the last two thousand years, Bible teachers and students of eschatology have had some tough questions to answer. Though they were all looking for the Second Coming of Jesus Christ, the signs were not there to indicate they were in the season of His return. For example, with the Diaspora, or global scattering of the Jewish people, how and when would this last week of years begin? If the nation of Israel was scattered to the four winds, with whom would the coming prince make a covenant of peace? How would he put an end to sacrifice and offering at the Temple if no Temple existed? None of this would really make any sense until Jerusalem was again under Jewish rule, something that hadn't been true since Nebuchadnezzar conquered Jerusalem, and something that seemed impossible until World War II ended.

The answers to these questions would come thousands of years before the state of Israel would even be a glimmer in any Zionist's eye. Before Daniel was told of these seventy weeks, God spoke to Daniel's contemporary, Ezekiel, and described with incredible detail how Israel would one day arise from the bones of its past as a sign to the nations that the end of days was near.

As the Jews were marched out of the ruins of Jerusalem toward Babylon, Ezekiel prophesied that Israel would be reborn. Once the Messiah was cut off (crucified) and Jerusalem again destroyed, the next great tick on the clock of God's countdown would be the resurrection of Israel as a self-governing nation. No other Bible prophecy of the last days would matter until this key element was in place.

Considering this, there is no question that the greatest prophetic event of my generation—and really of the last two thousand years— was the reestablishment of the state of Israel in 1948. But that begs the question once again, "If Bible prophecy is accurate in foretelling Israel's rebirth, then what does it say will happen next?"

CHAPTER 2

THE DOMINOES BEGIN TO FALL AGAIN

*"For I will take you from the nations, gather you from all
the lands and bring you into your own land. Then I will
sprinkle clean water on you, and you will be clean. . . .
You will live in the land that I gave to your forefathers;
so you will be My people, and I will be your God."*

—EZEKIEL 36:24-25, 28

At the same time Jerusalem was conquered and destroyed
by Nebuchadnezzar and his troops were marching the people of Judah
into exile (c. 586 BC), Ezekiel recorded what are the 36th and 37th chapters of his book. Even as the last remnant of the descendants of Abraham
appeared to be passing into the obscurity of defeat and slavery—a fate
from which no other nation has ever arisen again—God was showing
Ezekiel that Israel would one day emerge from the *"dry bones"* of the desolate and deserted wasteland Palestine would become in their absence.
God assured them they would again become a self-governing nation in
the land, which He had given to their patriarch Abraham. It was a prophecy that would take nearly 2,500 years to realize.

Despite such a seemingly impossible feat given the length of time that had passed, Bible scholars held up Ezekiel's visions as proof that Israel would again be a nation in the generation before the Second Coming of Christ. This was echoed in 1844, more than a hundred years before it would happen and decades before there was a Zionist Movement. George Bush (not the recent president but the cousin of his great, great, great grandfather) wrote a thesis on the first fourteen verses of Ezekiel 37. Mr. Bush was a professor of Hebrew at New York City University. In his thesis, he stated that Ezekiel 37:1-14 said there would be:

> *a final recall of the Jewish race from their prolonged dispersion among the nations, and their reinstatement in the land of their covenanted heritage. . . . The announcements bear nothing more unequivocally on their face, than that this re-establishment in the land of Canaan shall be final and permanent.*[11]

He stated Ezekiel prophesied that Israel—which had not known self-rule since Nebuchadnezzar destroyed Jerusalem and had not had a significant population in the Holy Lands since 135 AD (they always had some presence in the land)—would again be populated primarily by Jews. They would not only return to their ancestral home, but they would also re-establish their government and restore a dry and barren expanse into a lush and fertile land.

Professor Bush believed "that we are now just upon the borders of that sublime crisis in Providence of which the restoration of the Jews to [Palestine], and their ingathering into the Church, is to be one of the prominent features."[12] He later went on to explain that, through some string of seemingly unremarkable and unconnected events,

> *The dispersed and downcast remnant shall, one
> after another, turn their faces to Zion, and in sparse
> and scattered bands find their way to the land of
> their fathers. Thus shall "bone come to his bone;"
> one Jew shall meet another, entering from different
> quarters of the globe upon the predestined soil of
> Palestine. Urged by different motives, the natives
> of Poland, Germany, Holland, Spain, Africa, and
> the East shall drop in, in scattered groups, to the
> cities of Judah, with the hope of depositing their
> bones in the tombs of their patriarch fathers.*[13]

He also stated,

> *When the Most High accordingly declares that
> he will bring the house of Israel into their own
> land, it does not follow that this will be effected by
> any miraculous interposition which will be recog-
> nized as such. Nothing more is implied than that it
> will be so ordered in Providence that motives will
> be furnished for such a return, appealing it may be
> to the worldly and selfish principles of the Jewish
> mind. It is by no means improbable that the affairs
> of the nations, or the progress of civilization, may
> take such a turn as to offer to the Jews the same
> carnal inducements to remove to [Palestine], as
> now prompt them to migrate to this country [the
> United States].*[14]

Though he didn't know exactly how, Professor Bush looked into
Ezekiel's prophecy and realized that before any vision of John from
the book of Revelation would become reality, Israel would have to be

reborn, and its capital would be Jerusalem, the city David called his own.

I remember discussing the importance of these prophecies with Benjamin Netanyahu when he was still the Israeli scholar who headed the Jonathan Institute in the late 1970s. He said,

> *The truth of the matter is that if it had not been for the prophetic promises about returning to our homeland, the Jewish people would not have survived. There is something about reading the statements of the prophets in the original Hebrew language—the powerful impact of those words bores deep into your heart and is implanted into your mind. There is absolutely no question but that those ancient prophetic promises kept hope alive in the hearts of Jewish people and sustained us over the generations when we had nothing else to cling to.*

Echoing Professor Bush's thesis, William E. Blackstone published his groundbreaking book, *Jesus Is Coming,* in 1887. Blackstone's book was so popular for so long that it was revised and republished nearly four decades later. In it, Reverend Blackstone lists scripture upon scripture that point to the restoration of Israel in the last days as part of God's divine plan for the Jewish people. He wrote, "At the first restoration [from Babylon, c. 536 BC] they [the Jews] returned to be overthrown and driven out again. But in the second, they will return and remain, no more to go out. They will be exalted and dwell in safety, and the Gentile nations will flow to them."[15]

Both these men, and others, have pointed to the rebirth of the nation of Israel as the entry point into the last generation of the Church. As I stated in my book, *The American Prophecies,* Jesus referred to the blossoming of the fig tree. The fig tree was used repeatedly by Bible prophets (see Jeremiah 24:5 and Hosea 9:10, for examples) as a symbol of Israel. Jesus said the blossoming of the fig tree was the sign that the end of the age of the Church was approaching: "*This generation* [the one that sees the sign of the fig tree] *will not pass away until all these things* [the signs of the end of the age] *take place*" (Matthew 24:34, inserts added).

If the rebirth of Israel on May 15, 1948, was indeed the blossoming of that prophetic fig tree, then those of us alive now are certainly in the generation that has seen its branch "*become tender and* [put] *forth its leaves*" (Matthew 24:32, insert added).

It is easy to see the picture of Israel's final rebirth painted in detail in Ezekiel's visions:

> "*Thus says the Lord GOD: On the day that I cleanse you from all your iniquities, I will cause the cities to be inhabited, and the waste places shall be rebuilt. And the land that was desolate shall be tilled, instead of being the desolation that it was in the sight of all who passed by. And they will say, 'This land that was desolate has become like the garden of Eden, and the waste and desolate and ruined cities are now fortified and inhabited.' Then the nations that are left all around you shall know that I am the LORD; I have rebuilt the ruined places and replanted that which was desolate. I am the LORD; I have spoken, and I will do it.*"
>
> *Ezekiel 36:33-36*

At the end of World War II, Palestine was in fact a desolate, forsaken wasteland. Since Israel's rebirth, that desert has flourished and bloomed just as these scriptures describe. Towns have been rebuilt and resettled, land has been tilled and become fertile, and the nation of

Israel has been fortified not with walls around the cities but behind a wall of nuclear deterrence. Because of that wall and her allies, Israel has not faced invasion since the attacks of Syria and Egypt during the Yom Kippur War in October 1973.

If the rebirth of Israel was the first of the events of the final days, what now?

WHAT COMES NEXT ON GOD'S TIMELINE?

After Israel's re-establishment, Ezekiel saw that the rejuvenated nation would be attacked by an ungodly alliance headed by "*Gog of the land of Magog*" (Ezekiel 38:2)—a coalition force thought to include Russia, Persia, Islamic states, and northern African nations. This battle is outlined in Ezekiel 38 and 39. Many Bible scholars believe that on God's prophetic countdown clock, this is the next domino to fall, and it may be the most significant event signaling the nearness of the end of the age. Bible teachers believe that what for centuries has been called "The Battle of Gog and Magog" will be the event that clears the way for the Antichrist to rise and form a one-world government. Soon after that, he will sign a peace accord with Israel, approve the rebuilding of the Temple in its historic location, and reconstruct the city of Babylon—beginning Daniel's Seventieth Week.

Of course, we must acknowledge that understanding and interpreting Bible prophecy is not an exact science by any stretch of the imagination. At best, God-given visions of the final stages of this age have come in scattered sound bites and fragmentary visions. It is like trying to piece together the lives of your great, great grandparents from old photos, journals, and letters you found in the attic years after they had passed away. Then take that and spread it between the interpretations of a dozen different writers, and you will get closer to the puzzle of eschatology. It has been left to us to piece together what was shown to Daniel, Ezekiel, Isaiah, Jeremiah, and Joel in visions, what Jesus told us in the Gospels, and what John saw in the book of Revelation, as well as all the snippets provided in the epistles and the chorus of other prophets in the Old Testament. Yet when you study this mosaic as long as I have, an overall pattern does emerge, a pattern that will inform us of approximately where we are in God's overall plan for humanity.

The closer we look at these prophecies, the more today's headlines and recent history start to echo the events foretold in the Scriptures. As we look at all these things together, prophetic events and details of how they might come about begin to fit into a logical, chronological order. As we sit with God's countdown clock paused at seven minutes until midnight, still in the Church Age, there are only a handful of events that could represent the next domino to fall:

1) the attack of Gog's coalition on Israel,

2) the Rapture of the Church,

3) the rise of the Antichrist,

4) the rebuilding of the Temple on the Temple Mount, or

5) **the Antichrist's covenant of peace with the nation of Israel.**

Whichever of these comes first, it seems very plausible that each of the others will follow in quick succession, very likely all within half a decade or less.

Of course, the exact order in which these will happen is still under debate by those who study end-time prophecy. Will the Gog coalition attack before or after the Rapture? Will Gog's attack be after the rise of a one-world government that creates a covenant of peace with Israel, or will Gog's attack be the catalyst for the rise of the one-world government? Will this war be the last gasp of desperate nations trying to hold onto self-rule in the face of a rising one-world superpower, or the first step in another Islamist attempt to destroy the influence of the United States and Israel?

As the exact details of when and how this attack will come about seem to perplex many, we can still see the gathering of the storm and the players coming into position. Even the motivations for such an attack on Israel are becoming clearer as the rhetoric of war and revolution in the Middle East climaxes.

Some have argued that the attack of Gog's coalition has to be in the initial years of the Antichrist's peace accord with Israel, because Israel has never had a time of peace and security since the U.N. approved the partitioning of Palestine into Jewish and Arab states on November 29, 1947. Some equate Gog's attack with the sounding of the sixth trumpet in Revelation 9:13-21, which speaks of an attack of 200 million horsemen from the east that kills one-third of the Earth's population with "*three plagues, by the fire and the smoke and the brimstone, which proceeded out of their mouths*" (Revelation 9:18).

Others—such as Tim LaHaye and Jerry Jenkins in their *Left Behind* series—put forth that this battle will be the inspiration for the peace accord that begins Daniel's Seventieth Week, and that it will happen prior to both the Rapture and the rise of the Antichrist. In his book, *The Coming Peace in the Middle East*, Tim LaHaye argues that the attack of Gog's coalition must happen at least three and a half years *before* the beginning of the Tribulation. Meanwhile, best-selling author Joel Rosenberg has placed the battle of Gog and Magog as the next milestone event of Bible prophecy in both his fiction and non-fiction books on the subject.

If the Battle of Gog and Magog is the next prophetic domino, then understanding this battle is crucial to knowing where we are in the last days of the Church Age. Yet before we explore that, we must first look at the other signs of the times that Jesus and Daniel gave us so that we can further verify our place on God's timeline. If you have read my other books, I am sure you are familiar with these as they are outlined in Matthew 24. However, since my last writings on this subject just a few years ago, facts that point to the appearance of these signs have changed exponentially. To understand the season, let's take another in-depth look for a better grasp of what we must do "*as you see the day drawing near*" (Hebrews 10:25).

PART TWO:

THE GENERATION
OF THE FIG TREE

"Be on guard, so that your hearts will
not be weighted down with dissipation
and drunkenness Son of Man."

—LUKE 21:34-36

CHAPTER 3

THE END
OF THE AGE

*The disciples came to Him privately, saying, "Tell us,
when will these things happen, and what will be the sign
of Your coming, and of the end of the age?"*

MATTHEW 24:3

Those born as the fig tree blossomed on May 15, 1948,
are sixty-four this year, and those who have seen its branches become
tender and shoot forth leaves are at least in their forties or fifties. Those
who were born the year Jerusalem came back under Jewish control will
be forty-five or older by the time they read this. While some have called
the generation that fought in World War II "The Greatest Generation"[16]
the world has yet known, it is not difficult to see that the generation that
has lived since the rebirth of Israel has seen the greatest acceleration of
change and quality of life in human history.

Because of the incredible advances in technology and the proliferation of communication since 1948, this generation has faced unprecedented mile markers. This has been the first generation for which

» world-citizenship is conceivable,

» the entire planet could be destroyed in war (now several
times over!),

» the world population has doubled and then tripled (from around 2.4 billion to 7 billion people),

» the average life expectancy of human beings has increased by more than twenty percent,

» families have gone from one rotary dial phone tethered to the wall to every member having their own cell phone, from which they can call almost anywhere in the world from almost anywhere else in the world, and,

» people can travel from one continent to another in hours instead of weeks.

When a vision of the end times was given to Daniel in the last three chapters of his book, he was told to seal it up for the generation in which *"many will go back and forth, and knowledge will increase"* (Daniel 12:4). No generation in the history of the world has traveled so much or seen knowledge increase so quickly as ours. From the birth of Jesus Christ to the invention of the steam engine, people largely traveled in the same way—it was virtually the same for Charles Dickens as it had been for Shakespeare or Caesar. Today, we can be anywhere in the world in hours and have even stepped from Earth to the moon within days.

What humanity knows, is inventing, or is discovering is increasing at an exponential rate. Computers have gone from machines that fill entire rooms to "smart phones" you can hold in your hand. The designers of the supercomputers of the 1940s could never have dreamed of this possibility. Topics that took months of research, traveling between libraries and paging through tomes of books, can now be exhausted in a few hours of surfing the Internet. Literally anything you want to know in the world is accessible through a few keystrokes or clicks of a mouse.

It is funny to think that in the 1890s, William Blackstone quoted Daniel 12:4 and spoke of how it was being fulfilled in his time. If Rev. Blackstone could see the fulfillment of the signs of Daniel 12 and Matthew

24 in his generation, how much more applicable are they to our time? Moreover, in Blackstone's time Zionism was in its infancy, and returning to the land of their fathers was little more than a pipe dream for the Jews. Even as sure as he was that Israel would be reborn, little could Blackstone have fathomed that it would come into existence in less than half a century later.

Today the fig tree has come to life, and the signs Jesus spoke of are happening all around us. As another decade dawns in the twenty-first century, it is worth reviewing these signs to see just how much more prominent they now are than they have ever been before.

THE GREATEST SERMON EVER GIVEN . . . PART ONE

Just as Ezekiel prophesied the future of Israel as the Jews were taken into Babylonian captivity, Jesus told what would happen at the end of the Church Age just before it began. He gave His famous "Olivet Discourse" (Matthew 24-25) just a few days after what Sir Robert Anderson believed marked the end of the sixty-ninth week of Daniel. What we now celebrate as Palm Sunday was the day—and the only time—Jesus allowed himself to be publically acknowledged as Messiah and King. The people lined the streets of Jerusalem waving palm fronds and crying,

> "*Hosanna to the Son of David;* Blessed is He who comes in the name of the Lord; *Hosanna in the highest!*"
> —*Matthew 21:9*

Immediately afterward, Jesus entered the Temple and chased the moneychangers away. That day and the next He confronted the hypocritical religious leaders to the point that they would never again challenge Him with their silly questions in public (Matthew 21 and 22). Then, after

He finished addressing the crowd in Matthew 23, He turned to His disciples and told them:

> *"Do you not see all these things [the Temple buildings]? Truly I say to you, not one stone here will be left upon another, which will not be torn down."*
> —*Matthew 24:2* [insert added]

He was, of course, referring to the prophecy of Daniel 9:26: "*The people of the prince who is to come will destroy the city and the sanctuary.*"

Even if they did not realize the reference, this had to have set the disciples to thinking about all they had experienced the past few days, from Jesus' triumphal entry into Jerusalem to His rebuking the corrupt Jewish leadership. Things seemed to be rising to some type of climax. Was Jesus ready to lead Israel to freedom from Roman rule and reestablish the throne of David? With thoughts of the days' activities and Jesus' prophecy about the Temple ringing in their ears, they decided it was the right time to ask Him the question that had been burning in their minds:

> *"Tell us, when will these things happen, and what will be the sign of Your coming, and of the end of the age?"*—*Matthew 24:3*

The age they spoke of was the one that began with the Babylonian conquest and would end with the re-establishment of Israel as an independent state. When would be the end of Israel's subjugation, the end of the disgrace of God's people? When was Jesus going to call Israel to arms and return it to world power? When was He going to set up His earthly kingdom? In essence they were asking, "Is now the time? Is this the end of the age? Is it today that a nation will be reborn in a day?" While they hoped that it was, Jesus didn't answer that part of the question. He didn't speak of what would happen in the next few days but what would happen centuries later, in the days just before the Tribulation, during the Tribulation, and then His Second Coming. He began to prophesy not to their generation, but to ours.

Jesus presented the signs of our time with the following instructions: *"See that you are not frightened, for those things must take place, but that is not yet the end"* (Matthew 24:6). He also wanted us to know: *"All these things are merely the beginning of birth pangs"* Matthew 24:8). So the following signs, which we are experiencing today, are not to scare us; and we are to remember they are only the beginning of difficulties that will increase and accelerate as we move toward the end of the Church Age:

1) *"Many will come in My name, saying, 'I am the Christ,' and will mislead many"* (Matthew 24:5),

2) *"You will be hearing of wars and rumors of wars"* (Matthew 24:6),

3) *"Nation will rise against nation, and kingdom against kingdom"* (Mathew 24:7),

4) *"In various places there will be famines and earthquakes"* (Matthew 24:7),

5) *"Then they will deliver you to tribulation, and will kill you, and you will be hated by all nations because of My name"* (Matthew 24:9),

6) *"Many will fall away and will betray one another and hate one another. Many false prophets will arise and will mislead many"* (Mathew 24:10-11),

7) *"Because lawlessness is increased, most people's love will grow cold"* (Matthew 24:12),

8) **"This gospel of the kingdom shall be preached in the whole world"** (**Matthew 24:14**).

After these have taken place, *"then the end will come"* (Matthew 24:14).

I believe *"the end"* Jesus describes in Matthew 24:14 is the end of the Church Age and the beginning of the Tribulation. The end is not His Second Coming, for He goes on to describe the Abomination of Desolation (Matthew 24:15), when the Antichrist desecrates a newly-rebuilt Jewish Temple. It is generally believed that the Church must be taken out in the Rapture for the Antichrist to come to power.

The Antichrist will defile the Temple halfway into the Tribulation. In Matthew 24:21-22, Jesus goes on to describe the second half of the Tribulation, called the Great Tribulation:

> *"For then there will be a great tribulation, such as has not occurred since the beginning of the world until now, nor ever will. Unless those days had been cut short, no life would have been saved; but for the sake of the elect those days will be cut short."*

Jesus prophesies *"the coming of the Son of Man"* (His Second Coming) in Matthew 24:27, 29-30 and the catching up of the saints who are saved during the Tribulation in Matthew 24:31. Then He goes back in time to describe the next great prophetic sign that would be seen in the Church Age: the blooming of the fig tree (the nation of Israel):

> *"Now learn the parable from the fig tree: when its branch has already become tender and puts forth its leaves, you know that summer is near; so, you too, when you see all these things, recognize that He is near, right at the door. Truly I say to you, this generation will not pass away until all these things take place."*
> *—Matthew 24:32-34*

Through many years of study, I do not believe Jesus presents all these events in the order in which they will happen. In my view, this is how the verses roll out chronologically:

1) Israel reborn as a nation and flourishes (Matthew 24:32-35)

2) The signs during the Church Age (Matthew 24:4-14)

3) The Rapture (Matthew 24:36-44)

4) The beginning of the Tribulation (Matthew 24:14)

5) The midpoint of the Tribulation and beginning of the second half, marked by the Abomination of Desolation (Matthew 24:15-20)

6) The second half of the Tribulation, called the Great Tribulation (Matthew 24:20-26)

7) The Second Coming of Jesus or Day of the Lord (Matthew 24:27-31)

8) The gathering together of those saved during the Tribulation (Matthew 24:31).

Of course, Jesus did not discuss these things in the above order, but I believe the reason for that was to first answer the disciples' questions about the signs, tell them what the ultimate end would look like, and then go back to address the Church Age, which was about to begin. He knew He was leaving in just a few days, and He wanted His followers to know what their purpose was, what should be occupying their minds and hearts, until He came to get them in the Rapture at the end of the age.

Of course, there is a good deal of debate about when the Rapture will take place, whether it will be before the Tribulation, in the midst of it, or at the end of it. Some believe that the gathering described in Matthew 24:31 is not just the Tribulation saints but all of the saints. Of course, much of this is a relatively recent debate, as the early Church fathers believed the Rapture would happen before the Tribulation began, as did most Bible teachers until the late 1800's.

When the post-tribulation Rapture theory emerged in the 1800's, William Blackstone attempted to turn Bible scholars back to early Church doctrine by writing *Jesus Is Coming*. In it he discusses the difference between the *Rapture* (when Christ comes for His Church before the Tribulation) and the *Revelation* (when Christ returns with His Church to begin His millennial kingdom). If you are interested in the exact timing and arguments for why the Rapture will be pre-Tribulation, I would suggest you read his book, particularly chapter 9, "Rapture and Revelation."

However, in this book I want to focus on the age Jesus describes in Matthew 24:4-14 and 24:32-44, the Church Age. This is our time and our generation, and we need to know what He says we will face and how we should respond. We *are* the fig tree generation that Jesus proclaims in the Olivet Discourse.

THE SPIRIT OF ANTICHRIST

In response to the disciples' question about the signs of the end of the age, Jesus first pointed out that the time before His return would be one of increasing hostility towards God. Many would arise to create kingdoms around themselves rather than see the kingdom of God expanded. To a greater or lesser degree, this is the spirit of antichrist, the attitude that says, "Follow me; I know the way; I will save you," rather than, "Salvation comes through Jesus alone."

The antichrist spirit is reflected in an attitude we find to some degree in our churches, as our leaders water down the Word of God for the sake of enlarging their congregations and followings, selling more products, and getting on more TV channels. We find it to a much greater extent encouraging the idea that salvation is found in governments, social movements, political parties, and even sports or artistic endeavors, rather than in seeking God. As Jesus put it:

> **"See to it that no one misleads you. For many will come in My name, saying, 'I am the Christ,' and will mislead many." —Matthew 24:3-5**

The last century and a half has seen the propagation of new religions and ideologies as never before. By mid-2004 research estimated that the world knew at least 10,600 distinct religions, up from only 1,000 different religions in 1900, and a number that will grow to over 15,000 by 2025, if Jesus doesn't return first.[17] That's a tenfold change in a century and an estimated fifteenfold change in a century and a quarter. And those figures do not include the 42,000 different denominations and paradenominations within the Christian faith alone (which is up from 34,000 only a decade ago).[18] Despite the fact that the world is approaching seven billion people, there are a surprising number of new "christs" out there, leading people either into new beliefs or to new interpretations of the Scriptures.

Starting in the 1970s and coming of age by the end of the twentieth century, a new field emerged in universities for the study of "new religions." Organizations such as the Center for Studies of New Religions (CESNUR) and *Nova Religio* have given a legitimate place in academia to the *thousands* of religions. The name "new religions" was adopted as this field grew, primarily because of the negative stigma of the term "cult." Of course, for academic reasons it is important to remove the negative stigma of groups such as The Peoples' Temple in Jonestown, Guyana, where some 900 members committed mass suicide; The Branch Davidians, who fought it out with local and federal law enforcement agencies in

Waco, Texas, in 1993; and those of the Heaven's Gate group, who committed suicide together in 1996. While these studies don't endorse such actions, they do embrace an attempt to understand all "legitimate belief systems," citing Voodoo and Wicca as legitimate religious studies and atheism and humanism as attempts to live in harmony with one another and the universe around us.

When Jesus warned that *"many will come in My name,"* He wasn't saying they would call themselves Jesus or Messiah necessarily, but that they would come proclaiming to be that for which His name stood. They would say they had been endowed with "the way" to Heaven or a new, never-before-known understanding of God. They would say they were children of God, as we are all children of God. On the other hand, they might say God doesn't exist, and would be embracing a lie. Just as Jesus said, *"I am the way, and the truth, and the life; no one comes to the Father but through Me"* (John 14:6), literally thousands are saying they are—or know—"the way" that no one else knows. Or they might say there are many ways, teaching a doctrine of universalism.

This false and deceptive worship can also occur in arenas besides religion. People build kingdoms in politics, the arts, news and media, education, sports, business, motivational speaking, or other fascinations that lift up individuals rather than God. To a greater or lesser degree these people come in all that the *name* Christ represents: the reputation, authority, or fame of an "anointed one"—someone with the favor of God especially upon them. By providing new ways of understanding the universe and salvation and making these beliefs unique to themselves, they claim what they preach is "a better way," better than any that has come before them, and certainly better than biblical Christianity.

Deception is a sign of our times. It is the tool of choice for predators seeking fame and fortune, who will take advantage of the innocent and hungry for God. Through elaborate cons and the manipulation of markets, they line their pockets with the wealth of nations. Others use the proliferation of anti-Christian or anti-Semitic philosophies to whip the masses into angry frenzies, attempting to topple governments and garner power for themselves. Meanwhile, a worldly Western culture, drunk on self-indulgence, entertainment, and consumerism, keeps many distracted from their responsibilities as God's manifest representatives to the rest of humanity. Others get sucked into personality cults or distractions that take God out of His rightful place of prominence in their lives.

Certainly many things in our culture are alright in their proper perspective, but deception and distraction have even turned things as harmless as sporting events, providing for your family, supporting a political party or leader, and listening to music into religions of their own. These are *"the worries of the world, and the deceitfulness of riches, and the desires for other things"* (Mark 4:19) that choke out the effectiveness of the Word of God in our lives. They are also the very things that will blind the masses to the precept that the season of Jesus' return is upon us.

Those wrapped up in such deceptions are liable to be like the virgins who did not prepare themselves for the bridegroom by bringing extra oil for their lamps. (See Matthew 25:1-13.) Though they may call themselves Christians, they are not. They will miss the Rapture because they never bothered to get to know the true Messiah, Jesus of Nazareth. As He warned in the Sermon on the Mount:

> *"Not everyone who says to Me, 'Lord, Lord,' will enter the kingdom of heaven, but he who does the will of My Father who is in heaven will enter. Many will say to Me on that day, 'Lord, Lord, did we not prophesy in Your name, and in Your name cast out demons, and in Your name perform many miracles?' And then I will declare to them, 'I never knew you; depart from Me, you who practice lawlessness.'"—Matthew 7:21-23*

LOSING MORAL FOCUS

I believe that in the 1960s America came to a crossroads which was marked by the assassinations of three prominent leaders: John F. Kennedy, Martin Luther King, Jr., and Robert Kennedy. When they were killed, America experienced a crisis of conscience. The United States was faced with the choice of repenting and crying out to God for His salvation or rebelling and becoming our own "saviors." Choosing the latter, you can see what a difference it has made. Just look at the statistics of what has happened in education, crime, government corruption, and national security since those days.

Taking prayer out of public schools (passed on Kennedy's watch), with Roe v. Wade in 1973, and teaching sex education in public schools (formally begun in the early 1980s but taught as early as the late 1950s and 1960s) quietly undermined our Judeo-Christian culture. These three things alone altered the moral fiber of America more than anything else. Secular humanism, abortion, and sexual immorality gained their foothold. Few understood the failure of the Church in America. We were deceived into thinking we were not expected to be salt and light in every area of human endeavor: education, media, the arts and entertainment, government, family life, business and technology, medicine, and public welfare.

Satan didn't just instigate the murders of the Kennedys and MLK Jr. in the sixties; in the ensuing years the American church stood by and watched as he took our witness of the Gospel out of public life. Now, we face a tremendous challenge to bring America back to God and biblical truth.

America has had some great advances in technology and medicine, but at the same time our world is more torn by war, terrorism, slavery, drug abuse, arms trafficking, child prostitution, political unrest, poverty and hunger, religious persecution, abortion, infidelity, divorce, and crime than it has ever been. Increased knowledge and technical innovation cannot replace moral clarity.

The belief has always been that invention and innovation would make life better for all, but instead it is putting new weapons in the hands of the selfish and manipulative. What should be getting better is only getting worse because we have lost the guidance of a national moral compass. When we can't determine magnetic north, let alone true north, we lose our way. We have lost the moral imperative that dictated our national conscience from the landing of the Pilgrims to the Civil Rights Movement of the 1950s and 60s. Certainly we haven't done everything right in our history, but throughout most of our past most citizens of the U.S. still had enough respect for God to see themselves as "one nation under God"— and time and again that helped us make course corrections when needed.

The events of Revelation are certainly coming with the ultimate manifestation of one Antichrist, but in the meantime the spirit of antichrist has been increasingly active throughout society. It influenced the dress rehearsals for the Tribulation that we have seen from the reign of Antiochus Epiphanes to the destruction of Jerusalem in 70 AD to the Holocaust during World War II. It is a life-hating, innocence-despising, truth-twisting, genocidal spirit that is all too alive and well in the world today.

While the signs of the spirit of antichrist are prevalent, we haven't seen the worst of it. Although this deadly influence is rising up to destroy the faithful and the innocent in our day, it has not yet shackled our liberty or our right to preach the Truth. We must continue to act for liberty and the protection of God's people everywhere, protecting as many as will listen from the growing confusion caused by this diabolical attitude and outlook.

Meanwhile, the Earth is groaning all the louder for the sons and daughters of God to fulfill their purposes. To understand the urgency of this, we must realize the other signs of the last generation are also intensifying. A new age is struggling to be born.

CHAPTER 4

BIRTH PANGS

*For the anxious longing of the creation waits eagerly
for the revealing of the sons of God. For the creation was
subjected to futility, not willingly, but because of
Him who subjected it, in hope that the creation itself
also will be set free from its slavery to corruption into
the freedom of the glory of the children of God.
For we know that the whole creation groans and suffers
the pains of childbirth together until now.*

—ROMANS 8:19-22

At 2:46 p.m. on the afternoon March 11, 2011, an earthquake measuring 8.9 on the Richter scale took place 231 miles northeast of Tokyo at a depth of 15.7 miles beneath the ocean floor. It was the fifth largest earthquake since 1900, when instruments to record the intensity of earthquakes first went into continual use. Only weeks earlier the world's attention was grabbed by an earthquake that devastated Christchurch, New Zealand, and killed more than 160 people. However, this earthquake outside of Japan proved to be over a thousand times more powerful, setting off tsunami alerts in more than fifty countries, as far away as the west coast of the United States.

The earthquake moved the main Japanese island of Honshu almost eight feet closer to the American coastline, changed the tilt of the Earth's axis by over six and a quarter inches, and displaced the water above it by several feet, creating a wave that rose to roughly thirty feet high by the time it made its way to the Japanese coastal town of Sendai. It took less than an hour to get there. The massive wall of water moved boats, cars, and trains like they were matchsticks, devastating homes, buildings, factories, bridges, railways, and highways as far as four miles inland.

Within hours, Japanese officials realized they would not only have to face the devastation to life and property but also the possibility of a nuclear meltdown in one or more of their power plants. The four plants nearest the epicenter of the quake were immediately closed down, but it was too late for the Fukushima Daiichi Nuclear Plant. Four of its six reactors exploded in the next several hours, leaking dangerous radiation across the region. The latest estimates as I write are that over 15,000 died, while close to 5,000 are still missing. I am sure those numbers will have changed by the time you read this.

For decades scientists have denied that earthquakes are increasing in number, saying they have been relatively constant throughout the Earth's history. The "press release" statement has been that it only seems like earthquakes are increasing since we did not begin monitoring them until 1900. However, recent events are beginning to make scientists question this. Of the ten largest earthquakes ever recorded (again, since 1900), three of them—the December 2004 tsunami quake in the Indian Ocean, the 2010 Chili quake, and this recent one off the shoreline of Japan—have all taken place in the last seven years. As one scientist put it: "What is clear is that for the 6.2 years since 2004, there have been more great earthquakes around the world than in any 6.2-year period throughout the 110-year history of seismic recordings. . . . The recent spurt of magnitude-8-plus earthquakes may be an extended aftershock sequence of the 2004 Sumatra earthquake."[19]

As you might expect, while believers point to such events and ask, "Could these be the events Jesus spoke of in Matthew 24 and the book of Revelation?" the secular media is already starting to call such thoughts lunacy. Take, for example, the recent rant of MSNBC's Lawrence O'Donnell:

> The book of Revelation is a work of fiction describing how a truly vicious God would bring about the end of the world. No half-smart, religious person actually believes the book of Revelation anymore. They are certain that their God would never turn into a malicious torturer and mass murderer beyond Hitler's wildest dreams.
>
> I know, and I know it with absolute certainly, that this absolutely is not—*is not*—the end of the world.
>
> I do know, I know, I really do know. I'm not kidding about this. I know it's not the end of the world. Listen to me . . . for the sake of your children and your grandchildren, listen to me: it is not the end of the world. [20]

The sides do indeed seem to be pushing to the extremes.

A TIME OF GREAT CHANGE

"*Pains of childbirth*" (Romans 8:22) is indeed an apt description of what the world saw in the opening decade of the twenty-first century. When a woman has a child, the contractions will occur sporadically at first and then come closer and closer together. As they happen more frequently, they also intensify. In the last century we have certainly seen things that looked like the signs Jesus foretold in Matthew 24, but not all at one time.

With that in mind, let's look at Matthew 24 again. Jesus didn't just give us one sign—He gave us several. In addition to warning us about the rise of false christs, He also warned us that:

"You will be hearing of wars and rumors of wars. See that you are not frightened, for those things must take place, but that is not yet the end. For nation will rise against nation, and kingdom against kingdom, and in various places there will be famines and earthquakes. But all these things are merely the beginning of birth pangs.

"Then they will deliver you to tribulation, and will kill you, and you will be hated by all nations because of My name."—Matthew 24:6-9

Midway through the last century we experienced World War II and Jewish persecution and genocide but not earthquakes. They were dress rehearsals for the time that was ahead. Then Israel became a nation and we had another sign: Jerusalem came under Jewish rule in the Six-day War. Another sign came shortly after that in 1973: Israel was on the verge of destruction from the Syrians and Egyptians and was miraculously saved in the Yom Kippur War—an echo of the war Ezekiel speaks of in chapters 38-39? Another dress rehearsal? Another birth pang?

Here an isolated sign, there an isolated sign—growing in frequency and intensity—echoes of what the Scriptures foretell will happen in the final days before the Tribulation begins. Today's headlines are aligning more and more with what the Bible prophets saw in their visions. At the same time, more and more are speaking about the "end of the age." Do you think maybe God is trying to tell us something?

As we entered this century, signs began piling up, one upon another, sometimes all at the same time, with growing intensity, just as birth pangs happen before a child is born.

» September 11, 2001 attacks and the War on Terrorism

» The financial meltdown of 2008 that has only worsened worldwide

» Natural disasters: earthquakes in Indonesia, Haiti, Japan, and elsewhere; Hurricane Katrina in the USA

» Grass-roots revolutions and civil wars sweeping the Middle East and North Africa

» Global Islamic threats against Israel and those aligned with her

The world has never seen a time when all of these signs happened so closely together as they are happening today. Just how close are we to Jesus' return?

With 24-hour news channels and the Internet, we are never far away from the "wars and rumors of war," the unrest, attacks, and rising hostilities between people groups around the world. In recent months we saw the governments of Tunisia and Egypt fall due to rioting in their streets. People turned out in droves, calling for freedom and an end to tyranny. Mobs of Iranian protesters were dispersed by tear gas, rubber bullets, and riot police in the streets of Tehran. Demonstrators calling for regime change clashed with authorities in Bahrain, Syria, and Yemen; and hundreds were killed. Jordan was threatened with similar protests that never really took root. Libya went from marches to civil war against the late Muammar Gaddafi, the unstable dictator who ruled that nation with an iron fist for over four decades.

Meanwhile, the U.S. continues its efforts to police Iraq and defeat Al-Qaeda in Afghanistan, even after finding and executing Osama bin Laden. Hezbollah has a majority control in Lebanon, HAMAS has the same in Gaza, and other terrorist groups continue to spew their rhetoric as Iran remains undaunted in its pursuit of a nuclear bomb. HAMAS and the Palestinian Authority have joined ranks, planning who knows what in response to the vote to unilaterally recognize a Palestinian state by the U.N. General Assembly. Abbas presented the petition to the United

Nations on September 23, 2011, but since then it has been in debate in the Security Council, though a decision may have been made by the time you read this. The U.S. has pledged to veto it, if necessary; however, they are hoping it will be rejected by a majority instead so that relations with Arab nations will not be further strained.

The bottom line is that while a Security Council veto would deny the Palestinians official member status, they appear to be fully committed to that demand. If the vote in the Security Council fails due to a U.S. veto or U.S. influence to get it denied by a majority of Security Council countries, the Palestinian Authority can still seek upgraded observer status at the General Assembly as a non-member state.

This could be interpreted as implicit U.N. recognition of Palestinian statehood because the assembly would be acknowledging that the Palestinians control an actual state. The advantage of this option is that it would require only a simple majority of the General Assembly, something rather easy to do with the vast majority of U.N. votes already controlled by the Arab bloc. If the Palestinians were to be recognized as a non-member state, they would be able to sign certain international treaties, such as the Rome Statute of the International Criminal Court, which they cannot currently sign. This would mean thousands of lawsuits against Israel and further isolation and demonization of the Jewish state.

Not only do we see nations rising against other nations now, but also kingdoms, proxies, and factions posture for clashes with their declared enemies. Islam versus the West, Shi'ites versus Sunnis, Arab Africans versus Black Africans—and, of course, those aligning themselves against Jews and Christians everywhere.

As for natural disasters, 2010 was the worst year on record in roughly a generation. "It just seemed like it was back-to-back and it came in waves," reported a U.S. Federal Emergency Management Agency (FEMA) official. "The term '100-year event' really lost its meaning."[21] The January earthquake in Port-au-Prince, Haiti, left more than 220,000 dead and millions without homes. In February an earthquake that was roughly 500 times as strong hit Chile and killed just under a thousand. There were also killer quakes in Turkey, China, and Indonesia. Overall, there were twenty quakes of 7.0 on the Richter scale or higher throughout the year.

Flooding in Pakistan killed just fewer than 17,000 and inundated 62,000 square miles. Russia experienced a record-setting heat wave that pushed temperatures up to 111 degrees Fahrenheit. In total, eighteen countries broke records for their hottest day ever, with Pakistan topping the list at 129 degrees. A volcano in Iceland shut down air travel in Europe for more than seven million people. Other volcanoes erupted in the Congo, Guatemala, Ecuador, Indonesia, and the Philippines. There was a tornado in New York City, something very rare, and a record two-pound hailstone with a diameter of eight inches fell in South Dakota.

From January to November 2010 almost 260,000 were killed in natural disasters, a stark contrast to the 115,000 killed by terrorists from 1968 to 2009. FEMA recorded a record number of natural disasters: seventy-nine—while the average number for a year is around thirty-four. The economic impact of these natural disasters for 2010 was in the neighborhood of $222 billion. And this doesn't take into account the British Petroleum oil spill in the Gulf of Mexico or the other man-made accidents that are having a greater and greater impact upon our planet. The Earth is indeed groaning with contractions.

Even if 2010 is an anomaly and natural disasters go back to around thirty-four a year, looking at these events still gives one pause. What will the future hold as our world population surpasses seven billion? At present, from 400 to 500 million people live in population centers near major fault lines. That's not only in California but also in Tehran, Algiers, and about a dozen other cities around the world. Furthermore, some of these cities are powered by nuclear plants. In the U.S. alone, there are now over 100 operational facilities.

The Indian Point Energy Center, about thirty-five miles north of Manhattan, is near a fault line, as are two reactors in California. One of these, Diablo Canyon, which lies between San Diego and Los Angeles, is actually near two fault lines. While it is built to withstand an earthquake with a magnitude of up to 7.5—which experts say is greater than any probable in the area—the plant is nearly four decades old. Even if earthquakes are not more frequent than they were centuries ago, they are certainly in the news more because they are causing higher and higher casualty rates due to the Earth's larger population.

Meanwhile, despite abundance in other places, famine and poverty plague roughly a third of the world's population. According to the World Bank, approximately 2.1 billion lived on less than $2 a day in 2008.

Did 2010 see an abnormal spike in disasters or a foreshadowing of things to come? The months of 2011 to date show the trend continuing: in the earthquake and tsunami that affected Japan; the devastating multiple-vortex tornado that struck Joplin, Missouri (it was already predicted to be the deadliest year for tornadoes in seventy-five years.[22]); and the earthquake that shook the Eastern seaboard within a few days of slighter rumblings in Colorado, followed just days later by devastating hurricane Irene. In the summer of 2011 much of the country was hit by a heat wave combined with a severe drought in much of the South. As a result, Texas has seen one of the most severe seasons of wildfires it has had in its history.

None of this on its own, of course, is conclusive evidence of the imminence of Jesus' return—after all, increased earthquakes, wars, and famines are just some of the signs. However, when we put all of the pieces together, the picture is overwhelming. As *Face the Nation*'s Bob Schieffer noted in his March 24, 2011, broadcast, in all of his fifty-four years as a news reporter, "I cannot recall an overload of news from so many places as we have experienced these last eleven weeks."[23] And almost all of these stories were of events that reflect what Jesus warned us about in Matthew 24:5-7.

Of course, Jesus also noted, *"that is not yet the end."* These were things that would happen in the time just prior to the beginning of the Tribulation. No doubt they will increase as we near the rise of *"the prince that is to come."* As these groanings and convulsions arise in the Earth and in the atmosphere, so they also seem to be arising between people groups.

ANTI-SEMITISM AND ANTI-CHRISTIAN SENTIMENTS GROW

Jesus warned as the end of the age approached:

> *"They will deliver you to tribulation, and will kill you, and you will be hated by all nations because of My name.—Matthew 24:9*

As I stated in my book, *The American Prophecies*, the greatest century to date of Christian persecution was not the first century but the twentieth. In the history of the world and of the nearly 69.6 million Christians martyred for their faith, over 65 percent were killed in the twentieth century.[24] That figure does not include how many Jews were murdered in the Holocaust and during other historical periods of attempted genocide. It is estimated that the first ten years of the twenty-first century saw another million Christians murdered for their faith.[25] Though this shows a significant decrease in martyrdom worldwide as compared to the twentieth century, it is still an alarming number. The truth of the matter is that while some of the most severe persecutors of Christians in recent history have eased their "cultural revolutions" to eradicate the "opiate" of religion—namely communist governments— those who profess faith in Jesus Christ still place their lives on the line every day throughout the Islamic world.

Though I could present numerous examples of this, one that has most recently come to my attention is the predicament of Aasia Noreen, a forty-five-year-old mother of five. In 2009 Aasia got into a disagreement with fellow field workers in her village of Ittan Wali, Pakistan, near the Indian border. The other workers were trying to pressure her into renouncing Christianity and becoming a Moslem. Aasia's family was the only Christian household in the village. Aasia, however, stood her ground, much to the chagrin of at least one of the other women, who also held a grudge against her for a past land dispute. To end the bickering, the wife of a village elder demanded Aasia fetch them water from a well in the Nankana Sahib district, several miles away. Aasia complied, but when she returned the disgruntled Moslem woman said it was sacrilegious to drink water collected by a non-Muslim. Aasia replied, "Are we not all humans?" The response brought another strong rebuke, and another argument broke out.

Shortly after, the disgruntled woman went to a local Moslem cleric and reported the incident. The cleric filed a report with the police on June 19, 2009, and on that same day the woman confronted Aasia in front of her home, accusing her of having defamed the name of Muhammad, saying she had denied that he was a prophet. Men working in the fields nearby overheard the quarrel, left what they were doing, and forced their way into Aasia's house. There they began torturing Aasia and her children, demanding she admit to blasphemy and repent. As things escalated, they tried to put a noose around her neck to hang her.[28] However, the police had been alerted by other neighbors and arrived just in time. They took Aasia into custody, supposedly for her own protection.

As more allegations were made, instead of being released, Aasia was charged with blasphemy under Section 295 C of the Pakistan Penal Code, a crime punishable by death. For over a year Aasia awaited trial, suffering the horrible conditions of a Pakistani prison, separated from her family and unable to work.

Finally, in November 2010 the accusations were presented before a judge. While the family hoped this would put the absurd matter behind them, instead of dismissing the charges as normally happened in such cases, the judge sentenced Aasia to death by hanging and fined her 100,000 rupees ($1,100). To make things worse, because many convicted in lower courts for blasphemy are threatened or even killed in prison before their appeals can be heard, Aasia was put into solitary confinement and all visiting rights were revoked.

The National Commission for Justice and Peace (NCJP) has said that up to 80 percent of blasphemy charges are filed to settle old grievances, which seems to be what was happening with Aasia as well. Until Aasia's case, most such convictions were quickly overturned in higher courts. It is believed that clerics and Islamic groups usually pressure local courts into making the convictions, then less intimidated courts overturn the rulings. The word of such cases travels fast, and generally angry mobs surround courthouses to chant slogans and demand the death sentence as trials take place, regardless of the facts, threatening violence if things don't go as they demand.

In Aasia's area, the local imam said he cried with joy when Aasia was sentenced to hang. He told reporters, "She'll be made to pay, one way or the other. . . . If the law punishes someone for blasphemy, and that person is pardoned or released, then we will take the law into our own hands."[27] No one has ever been executed by the government under this law, but many have been murdered after their release. Several Islamic groups have already taken to the streets of Pakistan to let the government know there will be anarchy if Aasia's sentence is not carried out. Since her sentencing, Aasia's family has had to go into hiding. At the end of November 2010, a hardline Islamic imam promised to pay $6,000 to anyone who killed Aasia.

While the sentencing has brought international protests, Aasia still remains in prison as of this writing. Even Pakistani government officials have been among those who have spoken out against the sentencing. Some have called for Aasia's pardon and protection by the president of

Pakistan at the risk of being targeted in the crosshairs of fundamentalists.

One who spoke out for Aasia was Punjab Governor Salman Taseer. Because of this, Taseer was assassinated by one of his bodyguards on January 4, 2011—shot down in cold blood in broad daylight. Several clerics and imams in Pakistan had called for Taseer's execution after his defense of Aasia. Different religious leaders offered a total of 50 million rupees ($579,300) for the assassination of Aasia and any who spoke out on her behalf. The call apparently worked. The bodyguard made no attempt at escape after gunning down Taseer, turning himself in to the police and telling them he had killed Taseer "because of the governor's opposition to Pakistan's blasphemy laws."[28] Roughly two months later, the Pakistani minister for religious minorities, Shahbaz Bhatti, who had also called for Aasia's pardon and opposed the blasphemy laws, was gunned down in his car.

What has happened to Aasia is unprecedented in many ways. The vast majority of such cases are quickly overturned, and Aasia is the first *woman* ever sentenced to be hanged for blasphemy. It might simply be labeled a new extreme. However, it is all the more frightening because of a resolution recently approved by the United Nations General Assembly. On December 21, 2010, despite ardent opposition by western states, non-Islamic nations, and human rights groups from around the world, a resolution entitled "Combating Defamation of Religions" passed by a vote of 79 in favor, 76 against, and 40 abstentions, with the Islamic block forming the vast majority of those in favor.[29]

Today in the United Nations General Assembly, the Muslim nations have a clear voting majority with 118 of the 192 countries aligned with them: 22 Arab League nations, 57 Organization of Islamic Countries, and the rest developing nations that are traditionally anti-American, anti-West, and anti-Israel. Right now, anything passed by the General Assembly carries only a declaratory weight, while the Security Council ultimately decides the actions and authority of the U.N. because of their

veto power. Should this change, as leaders like Mahmoud Ahmadinejad
seem to think it should, the future for Jews and Christians the world
over could turn dire quickly.

The Defamation of Religions Resolution has slowly gathered support over the last decade. It was first entitled "Combating Defamation
of Islam" when presented on behalf of the Organization of the Islamic
Conference (OIC) by Pakistan in 1999. The most recent draft is cleverly
worded "to promote and encourage universal respect for and observance
of all human rights and fundamental freedoms without distinction as to
race, sex, language, or religion."[30]

Despite initial appearances, at its core the resolution is actually *not*
for freedom and respect of all religions but endorses the rights of nations
to quiet dissenting voices within their borders with such laws as the one
that put Aasia on death row. It endorses the rights of states to limit freedom of speech and persecute minority religions for the sake of the state
religion. It gives sanction to the brutal use of Sharia Law, which calls for
criminals to lose their hands and women who are not veiled to be stoned
to death. According to Open Doors, an anti-persecution ministry started
by Brother Andrew to help oppressed Christians,

> If the Resolution became the basis for [internation-
> al] law, it would allow governments the power to deter-
> mine which religious views can and can't be expressed
> in their country, and the right to punish those who
> express "unacceptable" religious views as they see fit.
> So, in effect, it would make persecution legal.
>
> It aims to criminalize words or actions deemed to be
> against a particular religion, especially Islam. It has the
> effect of providing international legitimacy for national
> laws that punish blasphemy or otherwise ban criticism
> of a religion.[32]

Take the case of Aasia Noreen and multiply it by the million or more who are brought in for questioning, arrested, harassed, imprisoned, or attacked each year for their faith in Jesus Christ. In 2010, an estimated 100,000 were killed in such encounters, which is over 270 a day.[33] And this is in a world where secular and Christian human rights organizations are actively fighting this treatment. What will happen if such organizations are silenced, or *"in the twinkling of an eye"* (1 Corinthians 15:52) are suddenly gone?

Add to this the growing anti-Semitism and Islamification that is happening in Europe. As one Christian minister, who is working in Great Britain, recently told me: The front lines of the mission field are no longer in the third world but in the European nations. In recent months he has seen people lose their jobs for as little as saying "God bless you" to a Muslim or simply wearing a cross. These acts of "proselytizing" are being tolerated less and less, even in England, which was the birthplace of the Great Awakening and the Evangelical Movement. As Muslims relocate to Europe in ever-greater numbers, the pressure to institute tenets of Sharia Law is mushrooming in the European Union.

To make matters worse, attempts by state legislatures in Oklahoma, Tennessee, Alabama, and at least ten other states to ban Sharia Law from use in U.S. courts are meeting strong resistance. Pro-Islamic groups are currently challenging in federal court a recently passed Oklahoma law banning Sharia Law. In Tennessee, where the legislature is still debating a similar bill, protestors gathered on the steps of their capital building, calling for the bill's defeat. Though the legislation is focused on better enabling law enforcement to deal with terrorism, demonstrators claim the bill is trying to make it illegal to be a Muslim. In Alabama, a similar measure aimed at protecting future generations from an erosion of constitutional rights through the use of Sharia Law is also raising ire.

It is interesting that attempts to protect Americans from extremist doctrines is meeting with such animosity and volatile rhetoric even in heartland states. If measures to limit the activities of terrorist groups within our borders are being met with resistance from moderate Muslims, is it merely a misunderstanding or another example of kingdom rising against kingdom? Is the legislation as misguided as its critics say, or is there some other spirit behind the disputes?

PUNDITS, PAWNS, AND PROXIES

Revolution and war in the Middle East...natural disasters...persecution of Christians and Jews—all these are certainly evidence of the budding leaves of Matthew 24's fig tree. It is not difficult to read between the lines and hear the voices aligning the pieces of a prophetic chessboard for the next great clash of civilizations. The very ground beneath our feet rumbles awaiting the manifestation of God's plan for the Earth—one that will deliver peace for all, take the blinders off the eyes of those who love Him, and expose plans of evil for what they really are. When Jesus returns, war will end for a thousand years, and those who have proven themselves capable of manifesting His purpose in their lives will have the responsibility of putting back together a world torn apart by hatred, greed, and gluttonous over-consumption.

In the meantime, despite the confusion and deception we face, everyone will receive a chance to decide for themselves if they want to embrace the Truth or try to escape the justice of God. In the coming days, as the darkness gets murkier, so will the light grow brighter. There will be no more fence-sitting as the Rapture of the Church approaches; for even as the persecution increases, so will the work of the Holy Spirit to empower believers as witnesses for Jesus Christ. How do we know this?

The next prophetic sign of Matthew 24 is that before Daniel's Seventieth Week begins, the Gospel will be preached throughout the Earth. Even as those who are only nominal in their faith fall into apostasy, the world will see the greatest revival that has ever taken place. The great divorce that happened as Hell rebelled against Heaven will be played out on the Earth in the days to come, as people choose to serve Satan or Jesus.

What will people do as God once again shows Himself strong on behalf of those who love Him?

CHAPTER 5

THE GREAT DIVORCE

"At that time many will fall away and will betray one another and hate one another. Many false prophets will arise and will mislead many. Because lawlessness is increased, most people's love will grow cold. But the one who endures to the end, he will be saved. This gospel of the kingdom shall be preached in the whole world as a testimony to all the nations, and then the end will come."

—MATTHEW 24:10-14

To further triangulate the signs of the final days before Jesus' return, He said that alongside increasing persecution there would be a great falling away from the Church and the values of Christianity. This is the "great divorce" that all of us want to avoid!

At the same time, Jesus said there would be a growing witness for Him wherever believers allowed the Holy Spirit to speak through them, especially when they were called on the carpet for their faith in Him. More and more, people would face Peter's dilemma: Confronted because of their faith, would they proclaim Jesus as Lord and Savior or would they hem and haw and then deny they ever knew the Man?

In the writings of Paul, this apostasy is the most prominent sign indicating Jesus is returning soon. He wrote to the Thessalonians:

Now we request you, brethren, with regard to the coming of our Lord Jesus Christ and our gathering together to Him, that you not be quickly shaken from your composure or be disturbed either by a spirit or a message or a letter as if from us, to the effect that the day of the Lord has come. Let no one in any way deceive you, for it will not come unless the apostasy comes first, and the man of lawlessness [the Antichrist] is revealed, the son of destruction, who opposes and exalts himself above every so-called god or object of worship, so that he takes his seat in the temple of God, displaying himself as being God.
—2 Thessalonians 2:1-4 (emphasis and insert added)

To Timothy, he further added:

But realize this, that in the last days difficult times will come. For men will be lovers of self, lovers of money, boastful, arrogant, revilers, disobedient to parents, ungrateful, unholy, unloving, irreconcilable, malicious gossips, without self-control, brutal, haters of good, treacherous, reckless, conceited, lovers of pleasure rather than lovers of God, holding to a form of godliness, although they have denied its power; avoid such men as these. For among them are those who enter into households and captivate weak women weighed down with sins, led on by various impulses, always learning and never able to come to the knowledge of the truth.

For the time will come when they will not endure sound doctrine; but wanting to have their ears tickled, they will accumulate for themselves teachers in accordance to their own desires, and will turn away their ears from the truth and will turn aside to myths.—2 Timothy 3:1-7; 4:3-4

We need to take a hard look at these scriptures to see whether or not we are in line with the truth. There is no saving grace in sitting in a pew each Sunday listening to sermons. Are we hearing the truth of the Word and applying it in our lives, doing what He has called us to do; or are we just looking for encouragement and something to ease our guilty consciences? Do we need assurance that despite our selfish lifestyle and sinful indulgences, we are still okay because God loves us all equally?

What is happening in our churches today? Are we being more influenced by our culture, which encourages complacency about godly things, or by the Gospel, which reminds us to fear God, "do justice, love kindness, and walk humbly with Him" (Micah 6:8)?

COMPLACENCY LEADS TO APOSTASY

In December of 2010, Barna Group Research released a report of what it called six megathemes that have been emerging in the Church in recent years. These trends were drawn from statements made during 5,000 interviews conducted throughout 2010. The Barna researchers summarized their conclusions as follows:

1. The Christian Church is becoming less theologically literate.

2. Christians are becoming more ingrown and less outreach-oriented.

3. Growing numbers of people are less interested in spiritual principles and more desirous of learning pragmatic solutions for life.

4. Among Christians, interest in participating in community action is escalating.

5. The postmodern insistence on tolerance is winning over the Christian Church.

6. The influence of Christianity on culture and indi-
   vidual lives is largely invisible.[33]

While some of this—namely more participation in community action—is good, the rest seems to suggest that we have a new generation arising within the Church that doesn't have a solid grasp of what it means to be a Christian. The difficulty is that as our churches have shifted to seeker-friendly, "emergent" services and community projects over community outreach programs, and its proclamation that Jesus is the only way to be reconciled with God is being rapidly diluted. In the report, the authors cited such examples as people recognizing Easter as a religious holiday but not really associating it with the resurrection of Jesus Christ. More and more the Holy Spirit has become a symbol of God's presence or power and much less a living, distinct member of the Trinity.

Faith and Christian responsibility are becoming less and less part of the American conversation, as there is a greater division in peoples' lives from what they do on Sundays and what they do the rest of the week. More within the Church are accepting the secular premise that Christianity has added little benefit to the world and that love means the absence of conflict and confrontation more than standing up for justice, defending the innocent, and holding dearly to what is right even if doing so is not comfortable, politically correct, or profitable.

For the upcoming generation in the Church, faith has to be practical more than life-altering—truth is relative more than it is absolute. "Realism" trumps righteousness. Prayer, reading the Bible regularly, living simply, and spending quiet times in contemplation to seek God are being replaced by a Gospel of intellectualism, materialism, success, and tolerance of evil. The Christian faith is growing more and more compartmentalized and superficial.

As this happens, Christianity is being highjacked into a therapy for inner healing, rebuilding of self-esteem, and a platform for political action rather than a life-transforming surrender of ego and willingness to get on our knees before God and make ourselves ready to do whatever He tells us to do. Church services have become more like motivational workshops for how to succeed in life rather than offering encouragement and a challenge to adhere to the uncompromising integrity that refuses to disobey God even if it hurts. Christianity is practiced as a grab-bag of pop philosophy rather than the impetus for radical transformation, both individually and corporately.

Handcuffed to the increasingly rapid treadmill of modern society, most Christians today are swept along on the tide of materialism, consumerism, and fiscal irresponsibility that is plaguing postmodern American culture as a whole. Statistics for divorce, cohabitation, and children born outside of wedlock are rising even as marital happiness is falling—and the stats are the same inside the Church as out. We are embracing the Christian messages of encouragement and God's approval of us rather than biting the bullet to make our relationships work.

Depressed and exhausted by today's pace and life's demands, we eat up the message of God's love preached to us, but then we nod off when that love calls for painful changes in our behavior or worldview. Christianity is now more of a rehabilitation process or success seminar than it is a call to save the world through "the *way, the truth, and the life*" (John 14:6, emphasis added).

This is one of the reasons I have remained so adamant over the years about the importance of being prepared for Jesus' return, giving pastors and teachers the latest information on how modern headlines align with Bible prophecy. We need to remember there is truly no greater message of encouragement than that of the return of Jesus Christ—the message that for centuries has been referred to as "The Blessed Hope." We cannot let ourselves fall into the trap of preaching only what is popular and practical in the Christian faith. We must stay dedicated to the message of living for the growth of God's kingdom rather than being at peace with— and coming under the spell of—an increasingly self-absorbed world.

A recent interview by Bill Hybels with Bono of U2—an icon of modern pop culture in many ways—made a rather insightful comment along these lines:

> *A lot of people are happy with "pie in the sky when they die," but I don't think that is what is our purpose. Our purpose is to bring Heaven to Earth in the micro as well as the macro. In every detail of our lives we should be trying to bring Heaven to Earth. Have the peace that passes understanding at the center of yourself, but do not be at peace with the world, because the world is not a happy place for most people who are living in it. The world is more malleable than you think. We can wrestle it from fools if we will.*[34]

While actions for social justice cannot replace the work of the Gospel, nor can checking to be sure every jot and tittle of what we believe is accurate replace putting God's love into action. The fruit of true preaching of the Gospel has always empowered social change *and* moral accountability. Regardless of what many postmodern pop secularists teach, this is the very thing that made America and Great Britain superpowers at the end of World War II. We had an ethical workforce that turned in a day's work for a day's pay, and though it was not universal by any means, people better understood the importance of doing what was right over doing what would profit them the most. Politicians didn't make decisions based primarily on how the public would receive their actions, but on what they knew to be moral and just.

Abraham Lincoln would be eaten alive by the media today for the "callous" way he spent American lives to secure the future of the Union. But he was a man who knew there were things more important than life itself, and that without them, suffering would be much greater. America became the world leader because, time and again, men and women who knew how to pray did what God told them to do. When they did this, our nation was shaken from complacency into action—and those actions affected their world and their times for the betterment of all.

The reason I mention this is not some great nostalgia for the days of my boyhood, but because of what will happen as apostasy and persecution increase in the days ahead. It is, in fact, something that is already happening today. As the West has grown increasingly intoxicated by its technology, entertainment, and creature comforts, something else has been happening in the world where the philosophy of "live and let live" is not so readily accepted. In short, while the love of God has been growing cold for many in Western churches, among Arabs and Jews many are wholeheartedly turning to Jesus as Lord and Savior.

THE RUMBLINGS OF THE LAST CHAPTER OF ACTS

The book of Acts did not end with a closing salutation or an amen, because it is the one book of the Bible that will not be finished until the Church is taken from the Earth. I believe that somewhere in Heaven the events of Christians throughout history are being recorded in the subsequent chapters of Acts, and one day, when we finally get to read about them, we will be amazed.

The greatest chapter of this book is still before us. I believe we soon will live in another time, when God is so near, we have but to ask once for His help and we will immediately have it. The last chapter of the book of Acts will be the last lap of the Church, and it will be our fastest and finest. The years of persecution that we will enter before the rise of the Antichrist will be met with the most powerful outpourings of the Holy Spirit the world has ever experienced.

Jesus preached that there was a purpose for rising persecutions in the days before His return: A new focus on the cost of discipleship, and those paying that price would be a witness to the world of His truth. Before the Rapture, the Gospel will be preached with the power and authority that was evident among the disciples after Pentecost. Look at what Jesus had to say in Mark's gospel about this:

> *"Be on your guard; for they will deliver you to the courts, and you will be flogged in the synagogues, and you will stand before governors and kings for My sake, as a testimony to them. The gospel must first be preached to all the nations. When they arrest you and hand you over, do not worry beforehand about what you are to say, but say whatever is given you in that hour; for it is not you who speak, but it is the Holy Spirit."—Mark 13:9-11*

In Luke, Jesus adds:

> *"They will lay their hands on you and will persecute you, delivering you to the synagogues and prisons, bringing you before kings and governors for My name's sake. It will lead to an opportunity for your testimony. So make up your minds not to prepare beforehand to defend yourselves; for I will give you utterance and wisdom which none of your opponents will be able to resist or refute."—Luke 21:12-15*

As I have said before, in the days before the rise of the Antichrist, as the dark gets darker, the light will also become brighter. Christians who give themselves fully to God will be the missionaries of God's final harvest before the Rapture and the beginning of the Tribulation. It will be a time unlike anything the Earth has seen before. It will be the book of Acts *cubed*. While complacency and worldliness blind some, others will see as they have never been able to—and the early tremors of this epoch revival are already shaking the Middle East. According to missionary Tom Doyle, "Jesus is reaching out to the people of the Middle East in a powerful way, and the people are responding in record numbers. Millions have given their lives to Jesus Christ in the last ten years. That's right—millions."[35]

Pastor Doyle points out that while some ten percent of the nearly 1.5 billion Muslims in the world are radical fundamentalists, as many as half of the rest have little interest in Islam at all, since they are Muslims by birth not by choice. After September 11 they were shocked and appalled by what extremists had done in the name of their faith, murdering innocent people in a war most Muslims wanted no part of. Turned off by the radical minority that made all Muslims look like criminals, they are not finding comfort in the Koran but in the teachings of Jesus.

As Joel Rosenberg wrote in his book, *Epicenter*,

> *Before September 11, 2001, there were only seventeen known followers of Christ in all of Afghanistan. Today [his book was published in 2006] Afghan Christian leaders tell me there are more than 10,000 believers in the country, and Afghan Muslims are open to hearing the gospel message like never before. Dozens of baptisms occur every week. People are snatching up Bibles and other Christian books as fast as they can be printed or brought into*

the country.[36]

A similar thing is happening in Iran. From the time of the Islamic revolution of 1979 until 2000, as many as 20,000 Muslims have converted to Christianity. The number of Christians in the country has gone from around 500 to an estimated 220,000 today. In a panel discussion moderated by Joel Rosenberg at the *Epicenter Conference 2011* in Jerusalem, Hormoz Sharlat, who runs a satellite television channel that beams the Gospel into Iran, described what was happening there:

> *You hear about Ahmadinejad planning to wipe Israel off the map and developing the nuclear bomb . . . but what you don't hear is that, in Iran, Islam is experiencing its greatest defeat in [its] history. . . . Millions of Iranians have rejected Islam in their hearts—not necessarily becoming Christian, but they have rejected [Islam], so they are open. . . . They say, "We have tried Islam for thirty years and it hasn't worked! It hasn't worked for me, it hasn't worked for my family, and look at my society." Iran is number one in drug addiction—hopelessness is amazing, that is why drug addiction and suicide are high.*[37]

According to an Iraqi pastor Mr. Rosenberg interviewed, since the fall of Saddam Hussein in Iraq, "People are being healed. Many of them. We don't have much experience with that, but we're seeing it happen anyway. . . . Muslims are seeing visions of Jesus Christ. He is coming to them and speaking to them, and they are repenting and giving their lives to Him."[38] More recently, one Iraqi pastor said this of what is happening in Iraq, "Virtually every single day—*every single day*—someone is coming and knocking on the door of a church . . . saying, 'I had a dream about Jesus. Please, can you help me?'"[39]

Tass Saada, a former PLO sniper who is now a pastor and evangelist among the Palestinians in Israel, told the following story from Gaza:

> *There's one guy in Gaza who was a HAMAS fighter.*
> *He had the [suicide bomber] belt about six years ago . . .*
> *ready to come to Israel and do his suicide operation.*
> *That night—the next morning he was going to come*
> *with the belt—that night, the Lord appeared to him.*
> *He told him, "What you are about to do is evil. I am*
> *Jesus. I am the way and the truth." And he woke up,*
> *and that light that was speaking to him was walking*
> *in his room still talking to him. He ran. He jumped out*
> *of his bed and ran out of the room. For two years he*
> *tried to get someone to tell him about who Jesus is. . . .*
> *Eventually God sent someone [and he accepted Jesus*
> *as his Savior and Lord].*[40]

There are more Muslims who have come to Jesus Christ in the last thirty or forty years than came to Him in the previous millennium.[41]

The world is also seeing an increase in the number of Jews who are accepting Jesus as the Messiah. While Jewish believers in Jesus numbered in the thousands in 1960, it is estimated that they number in the hundreds of thousands today. In Israel itself, the numbers have gone from less than 200 in 1967 to around 15,000 in recent years. Evangelist and worship leader Jordan Elias explained, "When revival breaks out on a national scale in Israel and the world sees it—it's going to be like life from the dead to the nations in regards to salvation. It will be the catalyst for the greatest revival to ever hit the planet."[42] Sounds like the dry bones coming to life in Ezekiel 37, doesn't it?

Executive Director of Jews for Jesus David Brickner says that because of the growing pressures in Israel—increased anti-Semitism, Iran's imminent nuclear threat, and the events of the times lining up more and more closely with the end-time prophecies of the Bible—young evangelists are finding a "great openness [to Jesus], especially among their own age group." Brickner affirms that hundreds are embracing Jesus as the Messiah. Ari and Shira Sorko-Ram, co-founders of Maoz Israel Ministries, say this movement is not just among young people, adding: "I believe that this is the time of the beginning of Israel's restoration spiritually, when new life will be breathed into the dry bones and a great and mighty spiritual army will rise up in Israel in this generation."[43]

At present Christianity is again the fastest growing religion in the world, while not long ago it was Islam. According to the research of David Barrett and Todd Johnson, Christianity is presently growing by about 83,000 people a day, an estimated 4,000 more people a day than Islam, which is second on the list.[44]

The end of the age will be a time of great revival that will likely either end in the Rapture or the rise of the Antichrist and his peace accord with Israel. It seems quite logical, as Tim LaHaye suggests in *The Coming Peace in the Middle East*, that some event will trigger this revival at least three and a half years *before* the beginning of the Tribulation (for reasons we will discuss later). The only prophetic event that fits that description would be the supernatural defeat of the Gog coalition when it attacks Israel. Such an exhibition of God's power would very likely turn the present stirrings of the Spirit into a full-blown revival in the Middle East and across the globe. As that happens, Jesus promises:

> *"Yet not a hair of your head will perish. By your endurance you will gain your lives."—Luke 21:18-19*

As the time of the Tribulation draws closer, there will be less and less room between those who love God and those who don't. It will be either radical faith or apostasy—living the Gospel of Jesus Christ or loving the ways of the world.

TO WHAT DO YOU PLEDGE YOUR LIFE?

In the days leading up to World War II in Germany, people had the choice laid plainly at their feet to either pledge their lives and allegiance to Adolph Hitler or to follow Jesus. Men such as Dietrich Bonheoffer and the members of his congregation of the Confessing Church refused to take the oath of allegiance to Hitler. Bonhoeffer even went so far as conspiring to assassinate the Führer. Adolph Hitler was without a doubt one of the most obvious manifestations of the spirit of antichrist we saw in the twentieth century. He hated the Jewish people and forced Christians to become either apostates or enemies of the state.

Similar things occurred in the Soviet Bloc countries following the war (over five million Christians died in Soviet labor camps and prisons). An estimated 224,000 were executed for refusing to deny Jesus in the killing fields of Cambodia and Vietnam between 1950 and 1975. During China's Cultural Revolution, an estimated 500,000 to 1 million believers were executed and 2.5 million imprisoned between 1950 and 1980.[45]

There is no question that in the generation since Israel became a nation, we have seen dress rehearsal after dress rehearsal for the Tribulation. We have but to read the writings of such men as Richard Wurmbrand, Watchman Nee, and Victor Frankl to begin to understand what it will be like for Christians and Jews as faith becomes outlawed in either a secular world or one controlled by Islamist fanatics.

Yet as that happens around the world, it will become increasingly evident for those not drunk on the Kool-Aid of liberal hypocrisy that the only true hope of salvation is in Christ Jesus. The person who "*endures until the end*" will know how to cling to Him for whatever is needed to live every day as a witness to His sovereignty, righteousness, and love. If we will endure in Him until the end, then we will not only be saved, but we will see many come with us to the Marriage Supper of the Lamb.

SO WHERE DOES THAT PUT US?

There is no question that if these signs are the leaves of the fig tree, they are indeed sprouting and spreading their blades to take in the sun. And they are no longer just budding haphazardly along the branches, but all are unfurling at an accelerating pace. I have no doubt that the generation that will see the Tribulation and the return of Jesus is on the Earth today.

Knowing that we live in a time of such incredible prophetic significance, just how far along are we in that generation? If the next great event is either the Rapture, the attack of Gog's coalition on Israel, or the revelation of the Antichrist, when will that event happen? And what will it look like? How will it affect the Earth?

It is apparent from Scripture that the beginning of Daniel's Seventieth Week is not set on the timeline in the same way that the coming of the Messiah was. In Matthew 24:20 Jesus tells us to *"pray that your flight will not be in the winter, or on a Sabbath,"* meaning that the time of these events depends at least in part on our prayers and intercessions for the peace of Jerusalem. In verse 14 He also said that, *"This gospel of the kingdom shall be preached in the whole world as a testimony to all the nations,* and then the end will come" (emphasis added). James echoes this when he writes:

> **Therefore be patient, brethren, until the coming of the Lord.** The farmer waits for the precious produce of the soil, *being patient about it, until it gets the early and late rains. You too be patient; strengthen your hearts, for the coming of the Lord is near.—James 5:7-8* [emphasis added]

When a farmer knows that his crops are almost ripe, he begins to patiently watch for the best day to begin harvesting in order to get the largest and healthiest yield. As he waits and watches the signs, he sharpens the pruning blades, cleans and preps the storage elevators, and does whatever else needs to be done around the farm so that when the time of harvest is ready, everything else will be as well.

Despite the nearness of the final week of years before Jesus' return, there are things we can do to change the impact of what happens during the Tribulation. We can pray for its timing and intercede for the regions of the Earth that will be hardest hit by the events of the book of Revelation. Despite the imminence of the wrath poured out on the Earth that John saw and recorded, we can influence whom it will affect by increasing the size of the revival that has already begun. We can pray that daylight lasts longer, so that a fuller harvest can be brought in. We can pray for the harvesters, and we can become better harvesters ourselves.

The time before the harvest is always one of the busiest on a farm, even though little may seem to be happening in the fields. We live in such a time, and there are things we should be doing to influence the events of the Middle East so that the Gospel can do its fullest work. Therefore, we must not become complacent and self-centered. As the great divorce between Heaven and Hell takes place, we must be sure we are, without question, on God's side. We must do the work God has called us to do with all the more conviction and be the powerful witnesses for Jesus Christ He has called us to be.

Before I go too much further discussing our role in these last days, I want to take a closer look at what is logically the next key event in God's prophetic countdown. We need to understand who the players are and what the events leading up to it might look like so that we can be ready when the day of harvest arrives.

PART THREE:

THE FINAL DRESS REHEARSAL FOR ARMAGEDDON

"Thus says the Lord God, 'On that day when My people Israel are living securely, will you not know it? You will come from your place out of the remote parts of the north, you and many peoples with you, all of them riding on horses, a great assembly and a mighty army; and you will come up against My people Israel like a cloud to cover the land. It shall come about in the last days that I will bring you against My land, so that the nations may know Me when I am sanctified through you before their eyes, O Gog.'"

—EZEKIEL 38:14-16

CHAPTER 6

THE CHANGING FACE
OF THE MIDDLE EAST

Here's what Iran is doing today. It's in Afghanistan;
it's in Iraq; it's in the Yemen; it's pretty much taken over
Lebanon; it's taken over Gaza; it's in the Horn of Africa;
it's even sending its tentacles to the Western Hemisphere,
penetrating Latin America. This is what Iran is doing
today without nuclear weapons. Imagine what they will
do tomorrow with nuclear weapons.

—BENJAMIN NETANYAHU
At the European Friends of Israel Conference
February 7, 2011[46]

From May 13-15, 2008, Israeli President Shimon Peres held the first "Facing Tomorrow" Conference commemorating the sixtieth anniversary of the declaration of the state of Israel. The conference brought together some of the greatest minds in the world today to discuss what the future would look like for the global community, the Jewish people, and the nation of Israel, as well as to celebrate the contributions Jews and Israel have made to humanity.

I had the good fortune to be permitted to attend along with such leaders and thinkers as President George W. Bush, former British Prime Minister Tony Blair, French Foreign Minister Bernard Kouchner, former President of the Soviet Union Mikhail Gorbachev, former United States

Secretary of State Dr. Henry Kissinger, former Czech Prime Minister Vaclav Havel, President of Georgia Mikheil Saakashvili, Nobel Laureate and author Elie Wiesel, Ambassadors Martin Indyk and Dennis Ross, *The New York Times* columnist Thomas L. Friedman, and Harvard Law School Professor Alan Dershowitz. Also in attendance were business luminaries such as Google founder Sergey Brinn, Facebook founder Mark Zuckerman, Chairman and CEO of News Corporation Rupert Murdoch, and Chairman Ratan Tata of the Tata Group.

Of the myriad of topics discussed at the conference, one I found particularly interesting concerned what the first wars of the twenty-first century would look like. The speakers believed they would come in four waves (and remember, this was in May of 2008):

1) An economic attack: In a world where a growing number of corporations have more money than countries and hundreds of billions of dollars can be transferred in seconds, calling in loans or putting pressure on heavily-indebted nations could have the effect of a stealth bomb on a national economy. In states that are heavily corrupted, the ability to bribe and make contributions to re-election funds can put politicians into the pockets of unscrupulous corporate moguls or wreak havoc on economies by manipulating their currencies or stock markets.

2) A cyber-war: With the incredible growth of the Internet as a source for news as well as virtually anything else you would like to know, media wars using the World Wide Web could turn the tide of opinion in a nation in mere hours. A battle for the hearts and minds of entire continents could be sparked through the focused attention of just a handful of

people making posts and writing blogs. Social media quickly becomes a means of organizing protests or voicing opinions otherwise suppressed in a state-controlled media. Not only that, but through the use of viruses there is the potential to bring networks, power and communication grids, and entire industries to a grinding halt.

3) Proxy wars: War would be sublet to outside parties. As happened in Korea and Vietnam, larger, richer nations could fight each other through other states and organizations. However, now it is no longer about superpowers and who has the largest arsenal, but about who has the money, who would be willing to use their arsenals at any cost, and who could best manipulate their puppets to get them to do what they want.

4) Boots on the ground: The final wave would be a conventional invasion of armed forces marching in to take control as an occupying army. If the first three waves went well, then this one would be nothing more than a formality, with just a few skirmishes of local resistance rather than all-out battles between national armed forces.

The first three phases of such a war would be virtually invisible—a "spirit war" to manipulate individuals like pawns. The idea would be to win their allegiance and participation through the speed of the Internet and work them up into frothing mobs who would take on tanks by their sheer numbers. As we have seen in the Middle East recently, such early phases could topple governments in days, and conventional fighting would only have to be a strategy of last resort.

Through World War II and even up until the Six-Day War in 1967, wars were won or lost depending on the ability of militaries to:

» communicate efficiently and without the enemy being able to intercept and decipher messages,

» move and mobilize troops quickly and secretly,

» concentrate force in specific areas without the enemy being able to effectively oppose them, and

» employ the element of surprise.

We watched as Iraq was liberated in 2003 and Hezbollah launched missiles into Israel in 2006. War is now a media event scrutinized by the world. Had the U.S. not had incredibly superior firepower and an iron will to see the battle to the end, Baghdad would never have been liberated. Even then, we won the war and subsequently lost the peace until President Bush agreed to send another 150,000 troops into the region. As playing fields become increasingly more level, who will win—the country with media and public opinion broadcasting its every move in real-time, or the dictator willing to send every last citizen of his country into the fray in order to realize his mad dreams?

The speakers at the conference stated that the more democratic and bureaucratic a nation, the more ineffective it would be in its responses to the waves of such invisible wars. Leaders would be paralyzed by media scrutiny as every step they took would be broadcast around the world the moment it occurred, accompanied by running commentary and criticism like some sort of sporting event. People would see things develop as they happened on their computers, smart phones, on network and cable news channels—or as they heard it on the radio, read articles and blogs, and read about it on their e-readers and tablet computers. Every action would be revealed immediately, and whether right or wrong, it would instantly be controversial.

Now fast-forward almost three years to where we are as I write these words. Look at what has happened in the world in the last thirty-some months:

» In the second half of 2008, the sub-prime mortgage industry bubble burst, creating an economic black hole that sucked profits from around the world to the tune of over $4 trillion. Liquidity problems on Wall Street froze credit needed for payrolls and went as far as to put workers in China out of jobs and into the streets. There was virtually no corner of the Earth that was not affected by the recession, and as we will discuss in a later chapter, we have yet to see the end result of this financial meltdown.

» Hezbollah, an Iranian-funded proxy, was able to form a majority government in the Lebanese parliament. The new prime minister of Lebanon has been hand-picked by the terrorist group—and Hezbollah is still the prime suspect for the assassination of Lebanon's last prime minister. HAMAS has effectively done the same thing in Gaza, joining with the Palestinian Authority in hopes of forming a national government with it in Gaza and the West Bank.

» WikiLeaks was able to obtain top-secret documents and communications from the United States and its embassies. Then it began systematically releasing these sensitive documents over the Internet, giving the U.S. diplomatic corps around the world a serious black eye, revealing sensitive information about U.S. strategies and potential actions, and exposing the corruption and lack of integrity of the governments that were home to these diplomats.

» Israeli intelligence was able to temporarily derail Iran's nuclear program twice—setting it back potentially years—not with an air strike but by using a computer virus. According to one official I spoke with, the Stuxnet worm that was loaded into the computers at Iran's Natanz facility was "more lethal than an ICBM. A direct [missile] hit on a centrifuge would not have done as much damage as this virus had done." The attack shut down from 5,000 to 6,000 of the estimated 10,000 centrifuges at Natanz, severely crippling Iran's ability to enrich plutonium to weapons-grade. Some speculate that Iran could have a nuclear device within months, others believe the earliest Iran will be able to produce a nuclear bomb is 2015. Experts have been amazed by the speed with which Iran has replaced the damaged P-1 centrifuges.

» Protests have rocked the Middle East, many of which were fueled and focused through social media sites. Tunisia's President Zine El Abidine Ben Ali stepped down and fled the country after protests erupted. This set off a wildfire of riots across northern Africa and the Middle East that spread to Egypt, Jordan, Yemen, Bahrain, Algeria, Libya, Iran, and Syria. Not long after Tunisia's government crumbled, Egyptian President Hosni Mubarak ceded power to the Egyptian military after thirty years in office. The scenario was eerily similar to the Shah stepping down from power in Iran in 1979. Google marketing executive Wael Ghonim is expected to release his book entitled *Revolution 2.0* in January 2012, about how he used Facebook and Twitter to organize the protests. Ghonim was an important organizer who was arrested and held by Egyptian authorities for twelve days. Many are calling it a "social media revolution."[47]

» Other nations have responded with force, primarily Bahrain, Syria, and Libya, and as of today thousands were killed in Libya as its civil war dragged on. Libyan leader Muammer Gaddafi pledged to fight to the death, stating that as he retaliated against the rebels, "Everything will burn."[48] Nevertheless, he was eventually forced to flee his compound in Tripoli and was later captured and killed by rebels. Saudi troops moved into Bahrain and helped quiet its Shi'ite majority, who were calling for reform there. As of this writing, over 1,500 have died in Syria, which has no qualms about repressing protests with violence. As the Assad government looks to be losing the battle, the U.S. and Israel fear what could happen if terrorists use the government's crumbling to get their hands on Syria's stockpiles of mustard gas, VX and Sarin gas, and missile and artillery systems.

These are all examples of the three waves of war that will precede a "boots-on-the-ground" invasion of another nation. If proxies can be installed democratically, as has been done with Hezbollah in Lebanon and HAMAS in Gaza, the victory need never go as far as invasion. The occupation will already have been accomplished with the ballot rather than the bullet. Never send a knight to do what a pawn can accomplish on its own!

The question about what will happen in Egypt, which was formerly Israel's strongest ally in the Middle East, may have been answered. Rebels attacked the Israeli embassy in Cairo, the Israeli ambassador and his family fled, and the embassy was looted. Still, we wonder: As Egypt's military now sits in control of the nation and the protestors are cleared from the streets, who will step into the vacuum of power? And will they restore peaceful relations with Israel? I believe it is unlikely.

Terrorist activities have increased in the Sinai, including attacks on a tourist bus along the border with Israel. We must remember that democracies do not happen just because people are given the right to vote. Don't forget that the current regime in Iran was "democratically" elected after a revolution that was not much different than what we just witnessed in Egypt. Also, Germans *elected* the National Socialists (Nazis) in the early 1930s, only to have their nation turned into a police state.

Will Egypt become a true democracy with a multiple-party system representing its diversity, or will it be a sham that hands power over to the Muslim Brotherhood and Sharia Law? Unfortunately the latter seems all too likely, with the Muslim Brotherhood being the most organized group coming out of the chaos. Will it step into power in Egypt as Hezbollah has done in Lebanon—getting a facelift from terrorist organization to political party, which has repeatedly happened in the last four decades? Will free republics emerge in Egypt and Tunisia, or will they become Islamist states with groups like Al-Qaeda or nations like Iran pulling their strings?

Moreover, are there more prophetic overtones to these uprisings? As we have already pointed out, Iranian President Mahmoud Ahmadinejad told a crowd in Tehran's *Azadi* (Freedom) Square, "The final move has begun. We are in the middle of a world revolution managed by this dear (Twelfth Imam). A great awakening is unfolding. One can witness the hand of Imam in managing it."[49] Ahmadinejad also told the crowd that the Mahdi was creating a new Middle East that would soon chase the United States and Israel from the region and then the world map.

Despite having no diplomatic ties with Egypt, Ahmadinejad welcomed the Egyptian revolution as a continuation of the Islamic

Revolution of 1979, whose thirty-second anniversary they were celebrating as he spoke. He said, "[The] Iranian nation is your friend and
it is your right to freely choose your path. [The] Iranian nation backs
this right of yours."[50] Throughout Tehran, people chanted "*Marg bar
Mubarak* (Death to Mubarak)!" "Egyptians, Tunisians, your uprisings are
just and we are with you!" and "Hosni Mubarak '*mubarak*' (congratula-
tions) on the uprising of your people!"

Just days later, Iranian forces cracked down hard on those who
tried to protest their oppressive government just as Egypt had done. So
much for freedom! Iranian authorities have learned from their past mistakes, now knowing how to head off such gatherings before they are able
to form. This time they proactively installed riot police at key meeting
points, shut down Internet and cell phone service at crucial times, and
used tear gas and rubber bullets to minimize the bloodshed that put Iran
under international scrutiny after its elections in 2009. Thus protests
there have been controlled, while others around the Middle East are still
shaking governments.

Given what Scripture foretells for Egypt, it certainly looks like
things will get worse before they get better. According to Isaiah:

> *"So I will incite Egyptians against Egyptians; And
> they will each fight against his brother and each against
> his neighbor, City against city and kingdom against
> kingdom. Moreover, I will deliver the Egyptians into the
> hand of a cruel master, And a mighty king will rule over
> them," declares the Lord GOD of hosts.—Isaiah 19:2,4*

While Bible teachers agree that this chapter of Isaiah is about the
end times for Egypt, it is hard to say how often it will face such a scenario before the return of Jesus. Isaiah 19 does not just speak of inner
turmoil and possible civil war, but that the waters of the Nile will dry

up, resulting in food shortages (Isaiah 19:7-8), that the country will be plagued with unemployment (Isaiah 19:15), and, "*The pillars of Egypt will be crushed; All the hired laborers will be grieved in soul*" (Isaiah 19:10). It goes on to say that foolish rulers will lead Egypt astray until the country trembles in dread. It seems likely this will be just before the Tribulation or during its initial years. This might be one of the reasons why Egypt is not part of Gog's attack on Israel as described in Ezekiel 38-39. At some point Egypt's inner turmoil will lead it into complete despair as a nation.

The good news is that from this despair Egypt will experience a great revival:

> *In that day there will be an altar to the LORD in the midst of the land of Egypt, and a pillar to the LORD near its border. It will become a sign and a witness to the LORD of hosts in the land of Egypt; for they will cry to the LORD because of oppressors, and He will send them a Savior and a Champion, and He will deliver them. Thus the LORD will make Himself known to Egypt, and the Egyptians will know the LORD in that day. They will even worship with sacrifice and offering, and will make a vow to the LORD and perform it. The LORD will strike Egypt, striking but healing; so they will return to the LORD, and He will respond to them and will heal them.*—Isaiah 19:19-22

Will this be part of the revival that sweeps the Earth before the Rapture, or the one that erupts after the Abomination of Desolation that marks the beginning of the Great Tribulation? The timeline is unclear on this, but it is certain Egypt has more to suffer before the Lord "will heal them."

While the exact outcome of the current unrest in these Islamic states is far from foreseeable at this point, one thing seems relatively certain: The new governments that arise in Tunisia and Egypt, if not elsewhere as this unrest continues, will be less friendly toward the West and more vulnerable to Iranian influence. Egypt has already allowed Iranian warships to cross through the Suez Canal into the Mediterranean, a "provocation" that had the Israeli navy on high alert. Those ships soon docked in the Syrian port of Latakia, supposedly preparing for "training exercises." This was the first time that Iranian ships were allowed to use the Canal since the Islamic Revolution of 1979,[51] and it sets an eerie precedent for who will be Egypt's allies in the future. Once again, a liberal U.S. president has fumbled a key ally in the Middle East; as Carter did with Iran in 1979, so Obama has done with Egypt in 2011.

While many around the world applaud the changes in these nations as victories toward more ethical, free, and democratic nations, these goals are far from being accomplished in the immediate aftermath of revolutions that used "tweets" and "posts" as bullets. No constitutions have yet been put forth, and the most organized parties waiting in the wings are not those with political platforms and plans for new governments but terrorist groups like the Muslim Brotherhood, hungry to create a new Sharia Law state.

Moreover, while government changes grabbed the headlines and the protests faded away, a Coptic church was burned to the ground in the Egyptian village of Sool, south of Cairo. A local imam had commanded his followers at Friday prayers to "kill the Christians because they had 'no right' to live in the village."[52] Thousands looted and attacked the building before setting it on fire. Members of the church fled for their lives during the night. No fire department came to put out the blaze, and the government plans to erect a mosque on that spot instead of allowing the Christians to rebuild. Even the modicum of religious freedom that existed under Mubarak's government seems to be fading fast.

While the world applauds what had been described as a grassroots move for freedom, what is emerging in Egypt is not a pro-western ally but something much more insidious.

SEEDING DARK CLOUDS

We need to realize that in refusing to support Mubarak, President Obama has humiliated a Muslim ally that has fought terrorism for decades, has supported U.S. policies in the Middle East, and has been one of the strongest allies of *our* strongest ally in the region, the state of Israel.

More than any other Middle Eastern leader, Mubarak was haunted by the ghost of Persia. Egypt was the first nation to offer the Shah refuge when he fled Iran on January 16, 1979. It was also the nation that provided his family with a burial plot for his earthly remains later that month, when no other Islamic nation would. Mubarak had witnessed the double-crosses, lies, and humiliation inflicted by the Carter administration on the Shah and his family.

While his government certainly had its weaknesses, Mubarak's dark side has been intentionally and repeatedly ignored by past presidents because of the hawkish foreign policy that necessitated strategic allies in the region, dictator or not. Now it appears President Obama does not consider America at war against Islamofascism, and there is no longer a need to undergird our allies. Instead, the Liberal-Left White House and press are deceiving the American people into thinking this is simply a battle between democracy and tyranny, not a battle to make certain we have a solid presence in the region.

We cannot ignore history without the risk of seeing events come back to bite us or sully our reputation as a nation. How could we so easily dismiss the ally we had in Mubarak and turn the country over to his sworn enemy, the Muslim Brotherhood? Despite its more recent facelifts, we need to remember what the Brotherhood has done in the past. They openly supported the assassination of Anwar Sadat. Hosni

Mubarak picked up the reins of government after Sadat's assassination and continued partnering in the region with the United States. Therefore Sheikh Rahman of the fanatical Islamist Muslim Brotherhood attempted to kill Mubarak. The plan was to kill the Egyptian president during a trip to New York City, on American soil. It was also Rahman, the blind cleric, who incited Muslims to "kill Americans wherever you find them; destroy their embassies, sink their ships, shoot down their planes."[53]

It was in a Cairo hellhole that Sheikh Rahman and al-Zawahiri began plotting to bring the U.S. to its knees by targeting the World Trade Center. Islamofascists from Egypt were trained and hardened on the battlefields of Afghanistan, where Al-Qaeda and Osama bin Laden provided training for the next generation of terrorists. One of the most well known would be Mohammed Atta, leader of the nineteen hijackers responsible for the 9/11 attacks on the World Trade Center, the Pentagon, and probably the White House (thwarted by courageous U.S. citizens, who gave their lives to save it).

Back in January 1979, General Robert Huyser, deputy commander-in-chief of the U.S Air Force in Europe, was sent to Iran to attempt to get the support of the Iranian military. After the fall of Iran, Huyser told me that President Carter had given him orders not to allow the military to support the Shah, to keep the military from a coup, and to garner support for the prime minister instead. For that, the U.S. would guarantee protection. Those generals were eventually brutally and mercilessly tortured and murdered when the U.S. pulled out of Iran and left them high and dry.

President Valery Giscard d'Estaing of France informed me that the overthrow of the Shah did not happen without the support of Jimmy Carter. It was on the French Republic Island of Guadeloupe in the Caribbean that he, West German Chancellor Helmut Schmidt, and British Prime Minister James Callaghan met with Carter. During that meeting, Carter told them that the U.S. had decided not to support the Shah's regime.

According to d'Estaing, Carter told them that Iran's military was going to take power and would bring order to the country. Many of the military leaders were pro-Western and most had been trained in the U.S. President d'Estaing said Carter "spoke very lightly of the man whom we had previously supported very strongly. [Carter] was a bastard of conscience, a moralist who treated with total lightness the fact of abandoning a man that we had supported together." For the sake of saving Iran from what he saw as the Shah's tyranny, he handed the nation over to Khomeini and his followers for decades of oppression far worse than anything the Shah had dreamt of doing. There is no doubt in my mind that President Obama is on the same course Jimmy Carter took. Should he choose not to heed wise council, the outcome may well be the same for Mr. Obama—he will hand Egypt into the hands of Islamic extremists even though his avowed hope was to help it become a democracy.

Those who live in genuine democracies loathe dictators and autocracies and harbor little sympathy for the likes of Egyptian President Hosni Mubarak—despite the fact that compared to the rest of the Muslim world, he is considered a reformer and has been reasonably loyal to America and especially to Israel. We so easily forget the lessons of the past: Democracy cannot be equated with freedom; it can allow for a mob mentality that puts evil men into positions they will not give up down the road. Some, like Mubarak, become our allies; others, like Khomeini, seek to destroy us.

After the Russians left Afghanistan, a poll was taken on who the Saudi Arabians would want for a president in a democratic election. Osama bin Laden won by a landslide. Recent polls in Egypt suggest that a powerful majority of its population would welcome a Sharia Law state. Seventy-seven percent of Egyptians want to see whippings and hands amputated for simple thefts, 84 percent are in favor of the death penalty for any Muslim changing their religion, and 82 percent approve of stoning as a penalty for adultery. About 60 percent of the Egyptian population supports the work of the Muslim Brotherhood—a rather strong majority before the first elections were even scheduled.[54] Fifty-four percent of Egyptians want the peace treaty with Israel scrapped,[55] and 95 percent of the Egyptians polled expressed passionate animus against the Jews. Meanwhile, a substantial minority admire Al-Qaeda, and many believe Ahmadinejad's allegation that the bombing of the Twin Towers was a CIA/Zionist plot engineered to discredit the Islamic world.

Is President Obama in bed with the Muslim Brotherhood just as Jimmy Carter was in bed with Khomeini before the overthrow of Iran? All is plausibly deniable at the moment, but the pattern of history is plain to see. Not only that, but President Obama joyously welcomed the Muslim Brotherhood to attend his February 2009 speech in Cairo and has maintained open channels of communication with them ever since.

A NEW MIDDLE EAST?

With Iran ready to play mother hen and gather all these fledgling new governments under her wing, the stage is set for a dangerous, eerie new alliance in the Middle East. I believe the long-term plan of the Islamists is to establish a Sunni caliphate in Cairo and a Shia caliphate in Tehran. Is that where we are heading while America sits idly by with its hands tied by the whims of the United Nations, without whose approval it now seems Barak Obama will do very little? If that happens, all those who gave their lives fighting terror in Iraq and Afghanistan will have died in vain in light of the damage that will eventually be done globally by fumbling Egypt just as we did Iran.

As if all of that were not chilling enough, the realignment of the loyalties in the Middle East has an even more foreboding threat. In the changing face of the Middle East, are we seeing the beginning of the Russian/Iranian-led coalition of nations foretold in the Scriptures? Is this the beginning of the army of nations unified against Israel discussed in Ezekiel 38 and 39 and the initial teetering of the next domino of Bible prophecy? Looking at how things are currently lining up, it is becoming harder and harder to deny this is so—and that Jesus Christ's return is not closer than anyone realizes.

CHAPTER 7

GOG'S MIGHTY ARMY

The sound of a report! Behold, it comes—
A great commotion out of the land of the north—
To make the cities of Judah
A desolation, a haunt of jackals.

JEREMIAH 10:22

In order to discover if the Battle of Gog and Magog is indeed the next tick on God's prophetic clock, we need to first understand what Ezekiel wrote to us about the attack on Israel that would be part of the end of the age. We must identify the players and the details of what is to happen, and then see how those fit with what we are seeing in today's headlines. In fact, every day seems to bring headlines that have prophetic implications. What exactly did Ezekiel see roughly 2,500 years ago when God showed him the final events of His divine plan for Israel?

A NEW AXIS OF EVIL?

Ezekiel 38-39 begins with God prophetically challenging *"Gog of the land of Magog, the prince of Rosh, Meshech and Tubal"* (Ezekiel 38:2). The challenge is not a friendly one. Through prophetic utterance, God is confronting Gog and this alliance of countries that include *"Persia [Iran], Cush [Ethiopia in many translations], and Put . . . Gomer and all his hordes, [and] Beth-togarmah from the uttermost parts of the north with all his hordes"* (Ezekiel 38:5-6 ESV). Whether Gog—*"the prince of Rosh, Meshech and Tubal"*[56]—is a human leader or the spirit over a region, such as were *"the prince of the kingdom of Persia"* and *"the prince of Greece"* in Daniel 10:13 and 20, is uncertain; although, most end-times-prophecy teachers point to him as being a human dictator.

The two "princes" of Persia and Greece appear to be fallen angels who delayed the angel that came to Daniel with a word from God during his twenty-one days of fasting. Since Gog is mentioned twice in Scripture—here in Ezekiel 38-39 and again in Revelation 20, which describes what takes place at the end of the Millennium—it seems likely Gog may not be a person but an anti-Semitic, antichrist spirit that stirs up hatred against God's people and probably has done so for many centuries. This may be the same spirit that was behind the events starting in Daniel 11:36, behind men such as Nero and Hitler, and those who will aid the Antichrist in his fight to destroy the Jews once and for all during the second half of the Tribulation.

Though the exact nature of Gog may be uncertain, the names Magog, Tubal, and Meshech point to the regions settled by the sons of Japheth, the third son of Noah (see Genesis 10:2 and 1 Chronicles 1:1-27). Magog, Tubal, and Meshech were grandsons of Noah who, according to tradition, settled their families in the lands north of the Black and Caspian Seas. Traditionally, these three are combined to represent the nation of Russia, with Meshech being the father of the settlement that came to be Moscow and Tubal the founder of the city of Tobolsk.

Tobolsk is north of Kazakhstan and Pakistan, on the western edge of the West Siberian Plain, about two hundred miles from the eastern foothills of the Ural Mountains. If you draw a line north and south through Tobolsk, the land west of that is home to the largest percentage of the Russian population, even though it is only about a third of the country. Tobolsk has a population of less than 100,000. It takes its name from the Tobol River, which flows north and slightly east from the southern end of the Urals. The city sits at the point where the Tobol flows into the Irtysh River, and from there it merges with the Ob and ultimately empties into the Arctic Ocean. The town is about 500 miles from the northernmost point of the Caspian Sea. I believe, as do many scholars, that Tobol derives its name directly from Noah's grandson, Tubal. This makes even more sense when you remember that Hebrew is an alphabet of consonants only, making Tobol and Tubal literally the same word.

The origin of Russia is a phenomenal, prophetic journey. Because if its size, it encountered constant tension on all sides: Asia, Europe, the Vikings, and the Slavs. That Russia's ancestors emerged from the sons of Noah has long been recognized, even by such men as the French philosopher Voltaire. As he wrote in *The Philosophical Dictionary*, "There is a genealogical tree of the events in this world. It is incontestable that . . . the Russians [descended] from Magog . . . one finds this genealogy in so many fat books!"[57]

The origin of the Slavs is a complete mystery to historians—not even enshrouded in legend. It is likely they were farmers in the Black Sea region before the Scythian invasions that took place around 700 BC. The earliest signs of nationalism in the region were south of Kiev (where my great grandfather was born), which seems to indicate these tribes were originally moving south to north. However, it wasn't until the ninth century AD, when the Vikings invaded, that the focal point of Russian culture moved up to Moscow.

Because of all this and other research we don't have space enough to include here, there is little debate among scholars of Bible prophecy that Magog, Tubal, and Meshech point to Russia as the lead nation of this coalition. They have believed this was true even though for centuries it seemed impossible.

When Cyrus Scofield published his famous study Bible in 1909, he included in his notes on Ezekiel 38 and 39 that Russia would invade Israel in the end times. That interpretation was challenged and even mocked. Many said, "How can you possibly say that? Russia is a Christian Orthodox nation, and Israel doesn't even exist . . . nor is there any possibility that Israel will exist." Scofield answered simply, "I don't understand it, and I can't explain it, but the Bible says it, and I believe it."

Today no one doubts that Russia might attack Israel—even unbelievers—especially since Russia has been known to regularly place Israeli cities in the crosshairs of nuclear missiles. It once stockpiled roughly $2 billion worth of weapons and equipment in southern Lebanon, which the Israeli army uncovered in a network of caves in 1982. Today Scofield's interpretation is generally taken for granted, even though for centuries it would have seemed ridiculous.

BITTER ENEMIES BECOME ALLIES

The shift in Russian regard for a Jewish state was to be followed by another occurrence that would have seemed impossible at the turn of the last century. Today, the strongest ally of Russia in the Middle East is undoubtedly Iran, the nation listed in Ezekiel as "Persia." The fact that Iran is modern-day Persia is certain. Its name was changed from "Persia" to "Iran" in 1935—and *Ērān* is actually the Middle Persian pronunciation of the name for the country. In 1971, the Shah of Iran held an enormous festival (costing an estimated $200 million) at the foot of the ruins of Persepolis[58] in southern Iran to commemorate the 2,500th anniversary of the Persian Empire, whose birth is dated to the same year Daniel had his vision of the Seventy Weeks.

Oddly enough, in the history of the world the last two decades represent the only time that Russia and Persia have been anywhere close to hospitable to each other. The two nations were almost constantly at war from 1722 to 1828. During that time Persia fought a war of attrition with Russia and Great Britain but never lost its independence as other nations in the region did, although it did lose a great deal of territory.

In 1925 Reza Khan overthrew the weakening Qajar Dynasty and proclaimed himself the first "Shah." He tried to model Persia after western industrialized nations, but because of its close ties with Germany at the time, Iran was again attacked by Russia and Great Britain in 1941. These Allied powers badly needed Iran's railroads to transport their war supplies. Following World War II, Iran remained closely tied to Great Britain and nearly became a constitutional democracy in the early 1950s. This, however, was thwarted by the United States and Great Britain in Operation Ajax, because the parliament wanted to wrest control of Iran's oil fields from British Petroleum.[59] Because of Operation Ajax, Iran's parliament was disbanded and the Shah became a dictator. This would be the West's greatest blunder in the Middle East until Jimmy Carter allowed the Shah to be deposed during the Islamic Revolution of 1979.[60] Until then, Iran had been a steadfast western ally, armed by the United States to be the fifth most powerful military in the world.

After the fall of the Shah, Iran was so embroiled in its war with Iraq from 1980 to 1988 that it had little time or energy for foreign relations. Considering all of this, the fact that Russia and Iran are now such close political bedfellows is unprecedented. This is the only time the world has ever seen cooperation, let alone open relations, between two empires that had been bitter enemies for centuries.

Cush and Put—as mentioned in Ezekiel 38:5— were sons of Ham, Noah's second son. According to Genesis 10, they traveled south into Northern Africa from the Ark's final resting place on Mount Ararat (Mount Ararat sits at the eastern edge of Turkey, against Turkey's borders with Iran and Armenia). Most scholars believe these two names represent at least the North African nations of Sudan, Libya, and Ethiopia.

Sudan has just voted to divide into two nations, a Muslim/Arab north and a Christian/African south. This was finalized on July 9, 2011. The Arab north—the nation was home to the birth of Al-Qaeda—would undoubtedly have no love for Israel. Not only that, but the Sudan has its own interesting history dealing with the "Mahdi," who chased the British from the region in the 1880s.[61]

Put's descendants populated the area west of Egypt, so today we would equate Put with the nations of modern Libya, Algeria, Tunisia, and Morocco, which are Islamic states. As we have already discussed, rioting and violence recently toppled Tunisia's government, and its immediate future is unclear. Egypt stands at a similar crossroads, and the civil war in Libya saw Gaddafi ousted, but has as yet produced no new leader. At the outset of hostilities there, Russia, Germany, and China initially stood with Gaddafi when the U.N. proposed a no-fly zone over the country to limit his attacks on the rebels. They later abstained when the vote for a no-fly zone was finally passed, and they subsequently refused to take part in enforcing it.

The last two on the list, Gomer and Beth-togarmah, are also mentioned in Genesis 10. Gomer is the eldest son of Japheth who, as we mentioned previously, was also the father of Magog, Tubal, and Meshesh. Togarmah—*Beth-togarmah* means "house of Togarmah"—was Gomer's third and last son. Gomer's descendants were called *Gi-mir-ra-a*, which the Greeks translated into "Cimmerians." A fair amount of ancient information exists regarding these Indo-European nomads, who were eventually driven out of Asia Minor northward through the Caucasus region (today the nations of Georgia, Azerbaijan, and Armenia) and into the steppes of southern Russia. They, like the descendants of Meshech, may have formed another central core of the Slavic race or, as some believe, were driven west to become eastern Europeans or Germans.

The Assyrians called *Beth-togarmah* "Til-garimmu," a name derived from the Hittite *Tegarama* and carried into classical times as *Gauraena*, or the town of *Gürün* in Turkey today. The Assyrians destroyed *Gauraena* in 695 BC. Because they were known for breeding and trading horses and mules in ancient times—"*From Beth-togarmah they exchanged horses, war horses, and mules for your wares*" (Ezekiel 27:14)—it is customary to associate the descendants of Beth-togarmah with the Cossacks of the Ukraine in southern Russia, who have long been world-famous horsemen.

A long-time ally of Israel, Turkey has slowly ended its ties with the Jewish state. Tensions between Ankara and Jerusalem continued to grow while Turkish Prime Minister Recep Erdogan openly courted Iran and welcomed the Islamization of his country. His move to join Brazil in an alliance with Iran, attempting to forestall further sanctions against Ahmadinejad's regime, was just one more link in the chain toward Islamic domination in Turkey. Most recently, the Turkish government expelled the Israeli ambassador and suspended all military agreements with Israel, demanding Israel's apology for intercepting the anti-Israel, "Free Gaza" flotilla launched from Turkey—even though it was backed by a Turkish terrorist organization. Of course, HAMAS and the Arab world are applauding Turkey's latest move against the Jewish nation.

Israeli Ambassador to the U.S. Michael Oren had been hopeful that Israel and Turkey would retain a relationship based on mutual respect:

> *Our policy has not changed but Turkey's policy has changed, very much, over the last few years. Under a different government with an Islamic orientation, Turkey has turned away from the West. We certainly do not have any desire in any further deterioration in our relations with the Turks. It's an important Middle Eastern power. It has been a friend in the past.*[62]

INTERESTED THIRD PARTIES?

Ezekiel 38:13 points to another group of nations and kingdoms:
> *"Sheba and Dedan and the merchants of Tarshish with all its villages will say to you [Gog], 'Have you*

*come to capture spoil? Have you assembled your com-
pany to seize plunder, to carry away silver and gold,
to take away cattle and goods, to capture great spoil?'"*

There is a great deal of debate about who Sheba, Dedan, and
Tarshish represent in this passage of Scripture, and I have found most of
it to be inconclusive. There is a Sheba and Dedan listed as great grandsons of Noah in Genesis 10:7, but also as grandsons of Abraham and
his concubine, Keturah, in Genesis 25:1-3. (These are repeated in the
genealogy in 1 Chronicles 1:9, 32-33.) While these references may be
helpful, the duplication does provide some confusion as to whether one
or either of these passages is relevant to what Ezekiel recorded.

However, earlier in the book of Ezekiel, Sheba, Dedan, and Tarshish
are mentioned as trading partners of Tyre, as are some of the other allies
of Gog. (See Ezekiel 27.) If this is the case, then all of them must have
been within caravan or sailing distance of Tyre, which is in the southern
part of modern-day Lebanon. Looking at maps of ancient times, Dedan
would be in modern-day Saudi Arabia, Sheba in or near Yemen, and
Tarshish is often considered as a European port in Spain or England. If
that were true, then the *"merchants of Tarshish"* would likely refer to a
trading alliance or economic union of western or European countries.
While some have tried to stretch this to include the United States as part
of its *"villages"* or colonies, this seems unlikely, though there is no way
of knowing.

If we accept this premise, and a Russian/Iranian coalition of proxies
were to attack Israel, Saudi Arabia and the other states of the Arabian
Peninsula—Jordan, Yemen, Oman, Qatar, Bahrain, The United Arab
Emirates, Kuwait, and even Iraq (which are largely Sunni Muslim nations
and are more friendly with the West)—would be unlikely to participate
in the attack on Israel. As a group, they and the West would be in a
place to question the Russo-Iranian coalition's motives and actions. If
the European Economic Union and/or the West as a whole were part of

Sheba and Dedan's challenge as the "*merchants of Tarshish with all its villages,*"[63] it seems more likely it would be something like the weak, initial protests that occurred after Gaddafi started attacking his own people in Libya. Either way, as the rest of Ezekiel 38 and 39 plays out, there isn't really enough time for Dedan, Sheba, and those of Tarshish to get involved in the skirmish before it will already be over.

WHO WILL THE PLAYERS BE?

In summary, those condemned by God in the initial verses of Ezekiel 38 for attacking Israel are a coalition of Russia, Iran, Northern African Islamic states, and perhaps Turkey. To add a modern update, they would likely also include Iran's proxies—Hezbollah and HAMAS—and the countries they occupy—Lebanon, Syria, and the Gaza Strip. As I write this, Syria is facing uprisings of its own that could change the face of that nation, just as Jordan has encountered in recent months.

In looking at who will be part of this coalition, it is important to note that Ezekiel was identifying people groups more than regions or countries. Subsequent migrations of these clans could easily make the anti-Israel coalition described here of a slightly different make-up. For example, it could also include some of the old Soviet satellite countries, other Islamic states, or even some European countries such as Germany, where some believe the descendants of Gomer ultimately settled. The bottom line is that with Russia's current alliance with Iran to develop its nuclear program and Iran's pledge to "wipe Israel off the face of the Earth," it is not difficult to see the two nations as architects of an attack to once and for all destroy Israel in the years, if not months, ahead.

The other key component of this prophecy is about those *not* participating: namely the nations of the Arabic Peninsula and the West. The fact that the Islamic states of the Arabian Peninsula are *not* part of this prophetic clash leaves them intact for what is to follow. For example, if

Russia and Iran are no longer influential players on the world stage after they are defeated—which seems likely following the destruction of their military forces—then what will happen once they are out of the equation? The United Nations could easily choose peaceful, rebuilt, and rejuvenated Iraq—the home of ancient Babylon—to be its new headquarters of operation in a Middle East that will be crying for peacekeeping forces to return it to stability. The destruction of Russia's and Iran's military muscle in the area would likely mean Saudi Arabia and Iraq would be the new Arab bullies on the block, and it would be time to rebuild Babylon as a world city and new center of power. If America does have a part in what happens in the book of Revelation, it may be the nation that helps pave the way for the new Babylon, which would be reestablished or rebuilt sometime before the events of Revelation 14.

The "Arab Awakening" makes this gathering prophetic storm all that much more disconcerting. Although the exact makeup of this Ezekiel 38-39 alliance is not completely evident as I write, it easily could be within the coming months. The one thing that seems certain, however, is that Russia and Iran will be driving the bus. With or without nuclear weapons, Iran has been itching for a fight with Israel for the last several years, and with Ahmadinejad's apocalyptic bent as a self-proclaimed prophet of the Twelfth Imam's return and his continued rhetoric about the end of the world being near, he is certainly positioning himself as the most dangerous anti-Semite the world has seen since Adolph Hitler.

We need to look more closely at what Ezekiel 38 and 39 say about this attack on Israel to better understand what all of this means. In this ancient passage, is there a clue for what we will be facing in the days ahead? How will Iran's development of the atomic bomb play into these events? What will motivate this attack, and what will the Middle East look like once it is over? How will Israel be affected? How will the U.S. and Europe be affected? How can we prepare for it? I believe the answers to these questions were indeed shown to Ezekiel, and that these events will play out very soon. As never before, we must

> *"Be on the alert—for you do not know when the master of the house is coming, whether in the evening, at midnight, or when the rooster crows, or in the morning— in case he should come suddenly and find you asleep. What I say to you I say to all, 'Be on the alert!'"*
> —Mark 13:35-37

CHAPTER 8

WHY ATTACK
ISRAEL?

"After many days you will be summoned; in the latter years
you will come into the land that is restored from the sword,
whose inhabitants have been gathered from many nations to
the mountains of Israel which had been a continual waste;
but its people were brought out from the nations, and they
are living securely, all of them. You will go up, you will
come like a storm; you will be like a cloud covering the
land, you and all your troops, and many peoples with you."

—EZEKIEL 38: 8-9

In late March of 2011, the world received access to a 28½-minute video reportedly approved by the highest levels of the Iranian government for release to the nations of Islam. It is entitled, *The Coming Is Upon Us*. In it, the Iranian clerics describe how the protests and revolutions of the "Arab Awakening" are all part of Islamic end-time prophecies according to the Hadith[64] (the most important set of Islamic writings after the Koran). The video mentions Egypt, Yemen, and other nations as specific examples. The Iranian leadership sees the governmental upheavals and civil war as signs that their ultimate victory is at hand—that the Twelfth Imam, the Mahdi, is at work and his appearance is near.

According to the video, it is foretold that in the last days Iran—"the people of the East"—will arise as a great power and begin the final jihad against the non-Muslim nations, most notably Israel, the United States, and Western Europe. According to their interpretation, it was foretold that the United States would attack Iraq as part of an overall war against Islam, that Iraq would become the center of world conflict, but that afterwards "it will serve as the capital of the world's governance by Imam Mahdi."[65] According to the Christian Broadcasting Network, the video also states:

> Iran's supreme leader, Ayatollah Khameini, and Hassan Nasrallah, leader of Iran's terrorist proxy Hezbollah, are hailed as pivotal end-times players, whose rise was predicted in Islamic scriptures.
>
> The same goes for Iran's President Mahmoud Ahmadinejad, who the video says will conquer Jerusalem prior to the Mahdi's coming.[66]

These men will "pass on the flag of Islam to the last messiah."[67] According to the teaching, the destruction of the Israeli regime and the liberation of Palestine will be the event that summons the return of the Mahdi and the beginning of a worldwide Islamic empire.

The video was released on the website of Reza Kahlil (a pseudonym), who once served as a CIA double agent within the Iranian Revolutionary Guard. According to Kahlil, the film was to be distributed throughout the Middle East with the hope of instigating further uprisings, all in pursuit of the Mahdi's soon return. The texts state: "The messiah will not arise unless fear, great earthquakes, and seditions take place, . . . The splitters will split and progress; the swift winged will attack, . . . Adultery will become common. Men will dress like women. Men will content themselves to men and woman to woman," and, "A Nation of the East will rise and prepare the way of the Coming of the Mahdi."[68]

In the same sequence, the video quoted the Hadith text: "The worst kinds of humans will become leaders," and showed pictures of George W. Bush, Ariel Sharon, Benjamin Netanyahu, and Barak Obama. The video foretells that the Muslim Brotherhood will come to power and help in the work of the Mahdi, and that the current poor health of Saudi King Abdullah bin Abdul Aziz, an Iranian rival, is also a sign of the last days: "Whoever guarantees the death of King Abdullah of Saudi Arabia, I will guarantee the immediate appearance of the Mahdi." According to Mr. Kahlil,

> *They show clearly in the movie that one of the most significant Hadiths that predicts this day calls for the destruction of Israel and the conquest of Jerusalem by Islamic forces as a last sign, which must take place before the Madhi reappears.*[69]

The video ends with the words: "I can tell you with utmost confidence: the promise of Allah for The Coming and the establishment of a new Islamic civilization is on its way . . . . Victory is near. Good tidings to the believers."

At two points in reading texts about the coming of Imam Madhi, the film shows a man riding on a white horse, eerily reminiscent of the breaking of the first seal in the book of Revelation:

> *Then I saw when the Lamb broke one of the seven seals, and I heard one of the four living creatures saying as with a voice of thunder, "Come." I looked, and behold, a white horse, and he who sat on it had a bow; and a crown was given to him, and he went out conquering and to conquer.—Revelation 6:1-2*

We cannot afford to ignore the signs. The world is already in a battle between two books, two faiths, and a diabolically contradictory set of prophecies for what will happen in the coming years. As Benjamin Netanyahu once asserted it in an interview:

> I would be careful to make an analogy between Judeo-Christian traditions and prophecies and the radical Islamic traditions ... The radical Islamists have a very violent tradition. In other words, it's not something that will happen, but it will happen by destruction *we* effect .... That is, we—the radical Muslims— should unsheathe our swords and embark on a great jihad of fire and blood ....
>
> [The Judeo-Christian tradition is] basically a benign conception of rebirth and redemption, as opposed to a very warlike cult of blood that seeks to destroy. It's construction versus destruction. It's peace versus war. It's beating your swords into plowshares as opposed to beating your plowshares into swords. And it's a very, very different conception.[70]

As we face the future, we must realize that Iran's vision of itself as the nation that must defeat Israel in order to facilitate the return of the Twelfth Imam is not simply some mad notion that will go away on its own. Iran has been arming itself for just such a clash of civilizations. It believes it is called by Allah to deliver the world from the Infidels, the Zionist regime, and their champions in the West. The proxies in Lebanon, Syria, and Gaza have primed for this coming war for years. With such antagonistic rhetoric flowing, it won't be long until Iran and Hezbollah take things into their own hands in order to be the instigators of the return of the Mahdi they have proclaimed themselves.

If Iran is not stopped, what plays out will look exactly like what Ezekiel 38 and 39 describes.

PEACE AND SECURITY

As Ezekiel hears it, God confronts Gog and his coalition for their evil intentions against the nation of Israel:

> *"It will come about on that day, that thoughts will come into your mind and you will devise an evil plan, and you will say, 'I will go up against the land of unwalled villages. I will go against those who are at rest, that live securely, all of them living without walls and having no bars or gates, to capture spoil and to seize plunder, to turn your hand against the waste places which are now inhabited, and against the people who are gathered from the nations, who have acquired cattle and goods, who live at the center of the world.'*
>
> *"Therefore prophesy, son of man, and say to Gog, 'Thus says the Lord God, "On that day when My people Israel are living securely, will you not know it?"* —Ezekiel 38: 10-12,14*

There are some telling conditions in the details of this prophecy that give us insight into how it will come about and just how close it might be. The first is that this will come in a time of relative peace and security for Israel, something the Jews haven't really known since the United Nations voted to partition Palestine into Jewish and Palestinian states in 1947. This is what has made some suggest that this attack will happen in the initial years of the Tribulation, soon after the peace accord engineered by the Antichrist, and that it is impossible any time before that. However, the initial years of the Tribulation don't appear to be any more secure than what Israel is experiencing now. Revelation tells us those years will be filled with natural disasters, wars, plagues, and famines that will kill a quarter of the world's population. (See Revelation 6:1-8.)

In contrast to this, Israel is certainly a nation of *"unwalled villages....* *living without walls and having no bars or gates."* Though it has had continued rocket attacks and suicide bombings even in recent months, it has not seen the threat of invasion since the Yom Kippur War of October 1973—almost four decades ago. Relatively, when not being openly rocketed, Israel is as much at rest and secure as it has been in a long time. There is no indication in Ezekiel's writings that this rest and security is something Israel experiences for a long period of time, though it must be long enough that Gog's coalition will see it as a window of opportunity in which to attack. A temporary settlement with the Palestinians could have produced such a window, and one was in the works, but was postponed. It could have been forced on Israel as early as the fall of 2011, after the U.N. General Assembly voted on unilaterally recognizing Palestine as a country—despite the Palestinians' unsuccessful negotiations with Israel.

If such a "peace" is brokered, the Quartet (Russia, The U.N., The E.U., and the United States) could unilaterally recognize Palestine as a state, with East Jerusalem as its capital. If the United States votes in favor of this move, it will pass. While at present President Obama has said he would veto such a plan if it came before the U.N. Security Council, how much influence he will have in stopping a vote in the U.N. General Assembly or convincing America's allies to oppose it is unclear. From recent speeches, he seems to be expecting some great concession from Israel, though he has yet to really specify what it might be. Could such a move create a time of peace and security for Israel that lasts until Gog's attack? As Paul described it:

> *While they are saying, "Peace and safety!" then*
> *destruction will come upon them suddenly like labor*
> *pains upon a woman with child, and they will not escape.*
> *—1 Thessalonians 5:3*

It will be interesting to see how this plays out in the months immediately ahead.

GREED

While Islamist animosity may seem enough to spur this attack, there is another reason for this invasion suggested by Ezekiel's writings:

> *"You will say, 'I will go up against the land . . . to capture spoil and to seize plunder . . . against the people who are gathered from the nations, who have acquired cattle and goods, who live at the center of the world.' Sheba and Dedan and the merchants of Tarshish with all its villages will say to you, 'Have you come to capture spoil? Have you assembled your company to seize plunder, to carry away silver and gold, to take away cattle and goods, to capture great spoil?'"—Ezekiel 38:11-13*

According to this, there are motives to this attack much more basic than the "liberation" of "occupied" Palestine. Gog's army will be coming to plunder and loot. But what will they be after—Israel's sheep and goats and whatever is in her treasuries? Israel is certainly much richer now than she has been for many centuries, but she doesn't have the ornamental riches of Saudi Arabia, Kuwait, Iraq, Iran, and other nations of the Arabian Peninsula. All of these countries have been wealthy due to one precise commodity that is getting dearer as the days go by: oil. If Israel were to discover large oil reserves, would that create the impetus for Gog to join Iran in trying to wipe the Zionist Regime from the map? Of course, we know that all of the oil in the Middle East is in the Islamic countries not Israel, right?

Wrong. Although the news has flown mostly under the radar, there are a handful of companies exploring for oil and natural gas in Israel and off its shoreline. Givot Olam Oil, which has been looking for oil in Israel since 1992, announced in August 2010 that it had discovered an estimated 1.525 billion barrels of oil accessible at its Rosh Ha'Ayin site, which is about ten miles inland from the coastline of Tel Aviv.[71] In November 2010, estimates were that the field was worth between $200 million and $900 million[72]—and at the time oil was only about $80 a barrel, more than 25 percent less than it is as I write. Of course, these are just the initial estimates at one site, and they are optimistically conservative at best. Testing of the sustainability of producing oil from this site continued through the summer of 2011, but serious oil revenues could begin rolling in before the end of 2012. Givot Olam is also drilling at other sites in this general vicinity, searching for other deposits.

In May of 2010, a U.S. Geological Survey report estimated there could be 1.7 billion barrels of recoverable oil and 122 trillion cubic feet of natural gas off the shoreline of the Levant Basin, most of which is within Israel's jurisdiction. The Levant Basin includes the Mediterranean trough off the coast of Israel, Lebanon, and Syria that goes almost all the way to the island of Cyprus. It also includes most of the Israeli mainland, the West Bank, western Lebanon, and the Syria coastal regions. John Brown of Zion Oil and Gas, which has exploration rights to a good deal of that area, estimated there is $917 billion worth of oil and gas (again at 2010 prices) in the region controlled by Israel.[73]

More recently, Houston-based Noble Energy—working with several Israeli partner companies—confirmed the finding of what has been dubbed the "Leviathan" natural gas field off the coast of Israel. Experts speculate that the Leviathan has at least sixteen trillion cubic feet of natural gas,[74] worth around $45 billion.[75] It is one of the largest deposits discovered in the last decade and could supply *all* of Israel's energy needs for the next century. As Noble and its partners start to extract that gas, Israel will go from a country dependent on the foreign import of coal and natural gas to being a player in *exporting* natural gas to the Mediterranean region—a remarkable turn-around for a country surrounded by oil and natural gas rich neighbors who are ill-disposed to trade fairly with Israel.

There is more. The Israeli stock market surged to an all-time high in the spring of 2011, up 130 percent since November of 2008, despite continued tensions in the region. If these discoveries pan out, Israel will certainly be supplied with enough "*silver and gold, . . . cattle and goods*" to make its neighbors envious!

Thus, the future is full of possibilities. As Israel begins to reap the benefits of these finds, its electrical plants will switch from burning coal to burning natural gas—a conversion that U.S. utility companies have found to be fairly straightforward—and end its dependence on foreign coal. And where does Israel get most of its coal? Seventy-one percent of Israel's coal comes from Russia.[76]

As the green revolution continues with the introduction of electric and natural gas vehicles, Israel could easily meet all of its own energy needs beginning as early as sometime in 2012. At the same time, it would likely begin to reap significant revenues from exporting these coveted resources. These exports would mean one of two things: 1) Israel could dramatically undercut the prices for these precious commodities to the chagrin of the other oil-rich states, or 2) Israel will see huge profits as prices continue to rise. Would Israel have enough of these resources to do this? Possibly. These are only estimates at this time, but considering that the concern for Libyan oil, which is only about 2 percent of the world's supply, sent prices over $100 a barrel as civil war began there, Israel's supplies could easily affect the world market. Even Israel's energy self-sufficiency would be enough to rock the boat. And with new discoveries in this vast region that have yet to be brought online, it won't be long before China and Europe start knocking on Israel's door, hungry to be better friends. Looking ahead to its future energy needs, China has left no stone unturned in negotiating deals for energy resources worldwide.

As for Russia, suddenly having an important consumer of its coal disappear and then finding it has to compete with that same tiny nation in selling "cleaner" natural gas resources to other nations will certainly sour their relationship even further. "*Magog*" will gain no new love for Israel. It might finally be time for Russia to deal with this nation that has been a thorn in its influence in the Middle East for more than a half century.

THE END OF THE AGE

I believe after reviewing these facts that this battle will mark the true beginning of the final days for the world as we know it. When this invasion takes place, we will either already be or soon will be in Daniel's Seventieth Week. At the end of the Tribulation, Jesus will return and set up His kingdom that will last a thousand years. The Millennium will be a time of peace, justice, and prosperity like the world has never known. The Battle of Gog and Magog will be the tipping point to all of the events described in the book of Revelation—very likely leading up to the Battle of Armageddon.

Many may then ask, "Why fight it? Why shouldn't we welcome God's end-time clock counting down to midnight so that Jesus can come again and come quickly? Isn't that the hope we should all be looking for?"

I find that an interesting question. In my life I have written many books on Bible prophecy and the political threats that could well be signs of it coming to pass, but I have no desire to see the world destroyed any more than God does. He, like a good farmer, is patient for the harvest. He wants the maximum number of people to be saved—He is willing to wait for the collection of "*the precious fruit of the earth*" (James 5:7 ESV). Though Evangelical Christians have been accused of madly wishing attacks on Israel because they will signal the return of our Messiah, I can tell you that simply isn't true. We have no design to instigate a nuclear war in the Middle East in the hope it will bring about the return of our Messiah. We are not "extremists" hoping for destruction; we instead hope *extreme* good will happen.

Certainly I can't wait to see my Savior face to face, but at the same time there are lots of things I feel I need to do before I meet Him at the Rapture. The reactions I get to what I teach tend to fall into one of two camps: 1) people get excited and start listening for the trumpets to sound, so that we can get out of this crazy world; or 2) they realize that it is time for the "*light of the world*" (Matthew 5:14) to shine brighter than ever. Unfortunately, there is usually an 80 percent/20 percent split in those reactions, with far too many in the first group and far too few in the second. It is my prayer that as you read this, you will be among those spurred to action, not those who want to collect all the canned food available and head for the hills to hold out for Jesus to come and rescue them.

For that reason, the "doomsday scenarios" I share with you in these chapters are but signs of the times. From what I am seeing and have seen over the last thirty-some years of being a correspondent on and advisor in the Middle East, we are truly on the cusp of Daniel's Seventieth Week, which is the Tribulation. As believers in Jesus Christ, this is important for us to know. These facts should be inspiration for us to act with renewed excitement about being Christians, to pray and act according to God's will as never before. Why? Because there is a great deal more for us to do before God calls us home.

Before we discuss that further, what will happen when Gog's coalition attacks Israel? How is that likely to play out? And what will the aftermath resemble? Let's take another look at the details God showed Ezekiel about this attack.

CHAPTER 9

BEFORE ARMAGEDDON THERE WILL BE HAMON-GOG

"You will come from your place out of the remote parts of the north, you and many peoples with you, all of them riding on horses, a great assembly and a mighty army; and you will come up against My people Israel like a cloud to cover the land. It shall come about in the last days that I will bring you against My land, so that the nations may know Me when I am sanctified through you before their eyes, O Gog.

"Behold, I am against you, O Gog, prince of Rosh, Meshech and Tubal; and I will turn you around, drive you on, take you up from the remotest parts of the north and bring you against the mountains of Israel. I will strike your bow from your left hand and dash down your arrows from your right hand. You will fall on the mountains of Israel, you and all your troops and the peoples who are with you; I will give you as food to every kind of predatory bird and beast of the field. You will fall on the open field; for it is I who have spoken."

Ezekiel 38:15-16; 39:1-5

I believe the Valley of Armageddon will host the final battle that will usher in the Second Coming of Jesus Christ. However, before that happens, another valley will see a fight of almost equal significance and devastation. It is this earlier battle—what has classically been called "the Battle of Gog and Magog"—or what I would call "the attack of Gog's coalition"—to which I now want to turn our attention.

The scriptures above tell us that Gog's army will come "*out of the remote parts of the north*" and "*like a cloud to cover the land*" coming "*against the mountains of Israel.*" If you look at a map of the terrain of Israel, you will see that the mountains of Israel fall primarily in two groups: 1) a range that runs down the spine of the nation west of the Jordan that includes the hills of Jerusalem, and 2) the Golan Heights. If an army were going to attack Israel from the north, it seems most likely it would come in through Syria and over the Golan Heights, especially if it is a land invasion, as happened when Syria attacked Israel in 1973. In fact, if an air attack were to launch from Russia itself, it would come over the Black Sea, through Turkish and Syrian airspace, and into Israel over the Golan Heights range.

There is no doubt that if this were the scenario, Gog would have learned the lessons of the last two wars with Israel and prepare accordingly. If there was anything learned from the Six-Day War of 1967, it was that Israel's air force is the tip of its spear, both offensively and defensively. Being a small country, Israel relies on its small forces on the ground to hold their positions until air support can arrive and eliminate any attackers.

In the Six-Day War, Israel was so certain Egypt, Syria, and Jordan were preparing to attack, that it struck first instead. The Israeli Air Force attacked so quickly and effectively that it allowed ground forces to move in with literally no threat from the air. Israeli tanks and armored divisions rolled through ground forces that were all but decimated. The lightning speed of the Israeli fighters shocked the world, and the victory was just short of miraculous.

In October of 1973, Egypt and Syria recognized Israel's air superiority, so they planned with that in mind. Instead of employing the same tactics the Israelis used to capture the Sinai Peninsula, the Golan Heights, and the West Bank, they instead kept their fronts with Israel at constant levels of mobilization, first fortifying one and then another, so that it was impossible to determine if there was a military buildup or just the moving and reorganizing of the same troops over and over again. Using this ruse, they snuck new armaments into the front lines, heavily arming their borders with Soviet anti-aircraft batteries and surface-to-air missile (SAM) installations.

Thus, when they launched their attack at 2:00 p.m. on the afternoon of Yom Kippur (October 6), ground troops invaded under an anti-aircraft shield that limited Israel's defensive capabilities to ground forces only. Their plan was to retake territory only as far as these shields could protect, dig in again, move the anti-aircraft shields forward, then advance once more under their protective umbrella. In this way they would inch forward until they regained the land they had lost in 1967.

The plan would have worked had not Israeli ground forces proved so incredibly formidable despite being completely outgunned. When you study the history of this fight, it is evident God protected Israel once again. In the Golan Heights alone, the Israeli army held out against roughly 1,400 tanks, 1,000 artillery pieces, and unchallenged air power with a mere 170 tanks and 70 artillery cannons.

Israel had only two brigades defending the entire region: the 7th in the north and the 188th in the south. These were stationed in seventeen fortified observation posts, primarily covering the two major routes through the Heights. A twenty-mile long, anti-tank trench ran from Mount Hermon to Rafid, and the Israeli Defense Forces (IDF) command felt that this would delay attackers long enough for Israeli air power to respond. Israel's tanks were positioned behind ramparts overlooking the Syrian valley floor that had once been called the Plains of Haouran.

The Golan Heights are really a network of receding plateaus more than a range of mountains. It is 480-square-miles of basalt tablelands that rise from a height of about six-hundred feet off the eastern edge of the Sea of Galilee to about 3,000 feet in the north along the southeastern border of Lebanon. These plateaus are scattered into a jigsaw puzzle of sharp escarpments and impassable canyons that severely limit the number of accessible routes leading through the Heights from the valleys of Syria into Israel's north. The spine of the Heights is made up of dormant volcanic cones, from which one can see both Damascus to the north and the Sea of Galilee to the southwest. When Syria held the Heights, it routinely shelled fishermen in Galilee and farmers in the Huleh Valley from secure and obscure positions.

The Syrian attack (which might give us a glimpse of what Gog's attack could look like) started with a massive shelling from all along the Syrian front and then a two-pronged ground assault. The northern attack came roughly along the road from Kuneitra to Damascus, and the southern prong crossed into Golan just north of Rafid. As defense of both positions called for airstrikes, the Israeli Air Force arrived. However, their initial attempts incurred so much damage from Syria's anti-aircraft shield, it was immediately evident that fighter jets were useless. It would take days before the IDF figured out how to effectively use its air power in this conflict, precious time they didn't have.

It must have been incredible to look through the sites of Israeli guns and watch this onslaught. They were taking out Syrian mine-clearing tanks, bridge-layers, armored personnel carriers (APCs), and tanks as fast as they could reload and shoot, but still the enemy kept coming. Nine hundred tanks were involved in Syria's initial attack, with another five hundred ready to move in behind once they broke through. Despite the best efforts of the Israeli gunners, the anti-tank trench was soon overwhelmed. The Israelis concentrated fire wherever bridges were built or the trench was filled in enough for tanks to cross over. The wreckage of Syrian tanks was mounting fast—and still they came.

As darkness fell, the Israelis didn't have the technology to match the Soviet night vision used by the Syrians, so they had to let the Syrians get close enough to see them in their searchlights before they could fire on them. Whenever a Syrian tank broke the line, Israeli tankers would swing their turrets, take out the interloper, and then turn their guns back toward the front again until they could find another target in their lights. The Syrians would break through, only to be pushed back. This happened over and over again as the hours of fighting continued during the next three days and nights.

By the afternoon of October 9th, Israel's 7th Brigade of the northern front was down to six tanks. As they fired their last rounds, realizing they would soon have to pull back or die, a small reinforcement of fifteen tanks came virtually out of nowhere to join the fight. Seeing the reinforcements and fearing they were the first of many to follow, the Syrians began to pull back to regroup. The fact was that these tanks were not reinforcements at all. It was a group of damaged tanks that had retreated and had been repaired! Those manning them were not fresh troops either. Some of them were returning to the fight injured from earlier battles. However, it was enough to throw the Syrians off and save the line from crumbling, at least for the time being.

The aftermath of this battle left the smoking hulks and scattered parts of some 260 Syrian tanks in the valley east of the initial escarpments of the Golan Heights. Along with them were the abandoned and destroyed APCs, mine-clearers, bridge-layers, artillery cannons, and the like. One Israeli colonel dubbed the wreckage "The Valley of Tears," and the name has stuck to this day.

Things in the south were worse, however. By October 9th the 188th was reduced to twelve tanks taking on 600. As night descended, the Israelis improvised, shooting illuminating rounds into the sky and using large xenon light projectors mounted on their tanks. They began using stopgap techniques, moving their tanks to one spot, firing several rounds, and then moving quickly to fire a few rounds from another position. In this way they hoped to convince the Syrians they were a much larger force, and that their defense was dug in.

One young lieutenant by the name of Zvi Gringold used these hit-and-run tactics to block the way of some fifty tanks from taking a direct route to the brigade's command center. After he had destroyed ten of their tanks, the Syrians became convinced the numbers they faced were too great and withdrew. In the next twenty-four hours, Gringold would take out some thirty tanks until injuries, burns, and exhaustion finally overcame him and he had to be evacuated.

The 188th fought bravely until the only tanks left were two trackless Centurions that had been rolled out of the repair depot. Foot soldiers fought at their side, firing bazookas and machine guns. Once those two tanks were destroyed, the Syrians, believing victory was near, took a few minutes to regroup. Their officers gathered to discuss the next phase of the advance. In the moments of that brief quiet, Israeli reservists rolled their tanks into position and found the Syrians milling around what had been the headquarters of the 188th. Before the Syrians could catch their breath, the Israeli reinforcements opened fire.

The precious minutes the last two tanks of the 188th had bought before they were destroyed allowed just enough time for reinforcements to arrive and turn the tide of battle. The vast Syrian incursion would be stopped far short of its goal and would be pushed back so far that Israel was ready to advance on Damascus when the ceasefire went into effect on October 23rd.[77]

If this historic war—as well as those in the Gulf in recent years—informs Gog's attack, it seems likely the Russo-Iranian alliance will want to neutralize both Israel's ground and air forces before it launches its attack, as well as create a similar cloud of confusion to mask its build-up for a ground invasion. Oddly enough, this could be the very thing Hezbollah and HAMAS have been preparing for during the last decade: experimenting to see how the IDF responds to continued rocket and mortar attacks from the confines of civilian population centers. Such attacks have been sporadic throughout the 2000s, with major clashes between Israel and Hezbollah in Lebanon in 2006, a forced blockade of Gaza by Israel and Egypt as HAMAS took control there in 2007, and a clash between Israel and HAMAS in Gaza in December of 2008. Some 95 percent of the roughly 4,000 rockets shot into Israel by Hezbollah in the 2006 conflict were fired from Russian Katyusha multiple rocket launchers. According to Israeli Ambassador to the U.S. Michael Oren,

> The Syrian and Iranian backed Hezbollah poses a very serious threat to the State of Israel. Hezbollah now has four times as many rockets as it did during the 2006 Lebanon War. These rockets are longer range. Every city in Israel is within range right now, including Eilat. They have bigger payloads; they are far more accurate. And we also know that Hezbollah has internalized the lessons of the Goldstone report. In 2006, many of their missiles were basically out in the open in silos and the Israeli Air Force was able to neutralize a great number of them. Today, those same missiles have been placed under hospitals, homes, and schools, because Hezbollah knows full well that if we try to defend ourselves against those missiles we will be branded as war criminals. So, Hezbollah and the situation in Southern Lebanon is of great concern to us and we're watching very vigilantly. We know that Hezbollah—in violation of U.N. resolutions—has once again penetrated southern Lebanon and transformed entire villages into armed camps and put in about 15,000 rockets along the Israeli border.[78]

For a number of reasons, it seems logical that if another invasion through the Golan Heights were planned with the help of Hezbollah, then the forces that would gather along the Syrian-Israeli border would do so under the cover of an even greater missile attack—the *"arrows from your right hand"* (Ezekiel 39:3)—perhaps even one coordinated with a simultaneous attack by HAMAS out of Gaza. At the same time, Palestinian terrorists would dispatch suicide bombers to Jerusalem—and wherever else they could—to wreak mayhem, stretching the resources of Israeli police, fire departments, military, hospitals, and other emergency response services.

Hampered by the threat of civilian casualties in the populated areas from which the attacks were launched, Israeli counterattacks would be measured and not taken unless pinpoint accuracy could be guaranteed. Gog's coalition would use long-range missiles to target key radar, communications, and power facilities to blind the Israelis even further to the real intent of the chaos. With ground forces also pounded in this manner along Golan, the invasion would begin rolling forth with air cover and paratroopers dropped in behind Israeli defensive lines to lead the way.

This attack would dwarf the attempted Syrian and Egyptian assault of 1973. Somehow, from the implications of these passages, Israel would be caught not only unprepared, but the initial hours of the attack would leave it relatively defenseless. Guided missiles would take out most of Israel's radar capabilities, the invading force would simply provide too many targets to stop, or some other combination of events would convince Israeli officials that there would be no way to stop the invasion. Israel would once again prepare its Samson Option, aiming its nuclear arsenal at Moscow, Damascus, Tehran, and other key cites, fully realizing the counterstrikes from Russia (and possibly Iran by that time) would put a final end to the dream that was the State of Israel.

TO GOD BE THE GLORY

As in 1973, in the coming battle against Gog those Israeli nuclear missiles will never be fired. Something like this is what will happen: As Gog's tanks begin to press into the Golan Heights, a massive earthquake will strike the region, tumbling the canyon walls of the Heights down upon Gog's forces in the same way the waters of the Red Sea once fell upon the Egyptians. Its tremors will be felt the world over. The guidance systems of Gog's aircraft, rockets, and missiles will suddenly become confused—due to some huge electromagnetic shift that occurs during the earthquake or some other factor that makes them lose their homing capabilities. Rather than traveling into Israel to strike their targets, Gog's fighter jets will fall to the ground on Gog's army, as if batted from the sky by God's hand.

The chemical or biological weapons housed in these projectiles (some of which were shipped out of Iraq into Syria the year before the Second Gulf War[79]) will decimate Gog's own troops. The topic of Syria's stockpiles of these weapons is in the press almost daily now as experts speculate about the future of the Assad regime with Syria's recent turmoil. In the ensuing confusion from these falling missiles, Gog's forces will likely turn upon each other, as happened with many of the armies that attacked Israel in Old Testament times. The devastation will make the Valley of Tears look like children's toys scattered across a bedroom floor in comparison.

Add to this the fact that if Iran should be allowed to develop the atomic bomb, the Sampson Option deterrent of Israel's nuclear weapons would be moot, especially for a suicide-bomber nation like Iran, which would gladly sacrifice its population to create "A World without Israel" and usher in the "perfect human being"—the Twelfth Imam—all bringing about the proliferation of Islam.

According to almost every military expert, within a decade of Iran developing the atomic bomb, we will have a nuclear "Armageddon" in the Middle East. That timeline is eerily close to Tim LaHaye's belief that we will only have a little more than a decade between the attack of Gog's coalition and Jesus Christ's return. I don't think any of the experts realize that this is no exaggeration. Once Iran has nuclear weapons, I can't see anything else stopping it from attacking Israel exactly as it is foretold in Ezekiel 38-39.

Ezekiel describes what God shows him will happen:

> *"In My zeal and in My blazing wrath I declare that on that day there will surely be a great earthquake in the land of Israel. The fish of the sea, the birds of the heavens, the beasts of the field, all the creeping things that creep on the earth, and all the men who are on the face of the earth will shake at My presence; the mountains also will be thrown down, the steep pathways will collapse and every wall will fall to the ground. I will call for a sword against him on all My mountains," declares the Lord GOD. "Every man's sword will be against his brother. With pestilence and with blood I will enter into judgment with him; and I will rain on him and on his troops, and on the many peoples who are with him, a torrential rain, with hailstones, fire and brimstone.*
>
> *"I will strike your bow from your left hand and dash down your arrows from your right hand [referring to aircraft, launchers, rockets, and missiles?]. You will fall on the mountains of Israel, you and all your troops and the peoples who are with you; I will give you as food to every kind of predatory bird and beast of the field.*
>
> *"On that day I will give Gog a burial ground there in Israel, the valley of those who pass by east of the sea, and it will block off those who would pass by. So they will bury Gog there with all his horde, and they will call it the valley*

*of Hamon-gog. For seven months the house of Israel will
be burying them in order to cleanse the land. Even all the
people of the land will bury them; and it will be to their renown
on the day that I glorify Myself," declares the Lord GOD.*
—Ezekiel 38:19-22; 39:3-4, 11-13 *[insert added]*

The defeat of Gog's army at the very moment of victory will be
so miraculous, providentially timed, and sudden, that the world will
recognize it was the power of God that delivered Israel. Joel 2:20 seems
to describe this defeat as well:

> *"But I will remove the northern army far from you, And
> I will drive it into a parched and desolate land, And its
> vanguard into the eastern sea, And its rear guard into the
> western sea. And its stench will arise and its foul smell will
> come up, For it has done great things."*

Certainly there will be detractors and skeptics who defend the
defeat of the Russo-Iranian coalition as a series of unfortunate events,
but that argument will only hold water with the most defiant opponents
of God's existence. Tremors of revival—which, as we have discussed, are
already being felt today—will sweep the Earth and grow until all true
believers in Jesus Christ are caught up in the Rapture.

As this revival is taking place, Israel will have years of cleanup work
to do. Some translations make reference to "The Valley of the Travelers"
in reference to where Hamon-gog will be. For example, in the *English
Standard Version*, Ezekiel 39:11 reads,

> *"On that day I will give to Gog a place for burial in
> Israel, the Valley of the Travelers, east of the sea. It will
> block the travelers, for there Gog and all his multitude will
> be buried. It will be called the Valley of Hamon-gog."*

It is believed that the Valley of the Travelers refers to the ancient trade route that spanned from Aqaba at the tip of the Red Sea in the south, through Petra and Amman east of the Dead Sea, the Jordan River, and the Sea of Galilee, all the way to Damascus. It was part of what was called "The King's Highway" or "The Desert Highway," and was referred to in Numbers 20. According to *The Treasury of Scriptural Knowledge*, the Valley of Hamon-Gog is

> *Probably the valley near the Sea of Gennesareth [Galilee], as the Targum renders, and so called because it was the great road by which the merchants and traders from Syria and other Eastern countries went into Egypt. Perhaps what is now called the plains of Haouran, south of Damascus.*[80]

The Plains of Haouran is a great expanse that includes the Valley of Tears; it is located east of the Golan Heights and the Sea of Galilee. Most of the debris from Gog's aircraft and missiles will fall on the troops gathered in this valley, while others will fall on the mountains of Jerusalem as far as they could penetrate before God intervenes.

After Gog's defeat, this valley will be impassible, possibly choked with toxins from chemical and biological weapons that will likely impact Damascus. (It is less than fifty miles from the Israeli border near the Golan Heights to Damascus.) The implication here is that after the battle, the devastated battlefield will become annexed by Israel as a burial ground. For seven months, workers in hazmat suits will walk this plain, gathering and burying the dead. The number buried there will be so many that the nearest village will be renamed "*Hamonah*" (Ezekiel 39:16)—which means "multitudes"—that will serve as a place of hotels and restaurants to care for those coming to visit the memorial cemetery. In the months beyond that,

"Then those who inhabit the cities of Israel will go out and make fires with the weapons and burn them, both shields and bucklers, bows and arrows, war clubs and spears, and for seven years they will make fires of them. They will not take wood from the field or gather firewood from the forests, for they will make fires with the weapons; and they will take the spoil of those who despoiled them and seize the plunder of those who plundered them," declares the Lord GOD.—Ezekiel 39:9-10

The nations that had sought to plunder Israel will instead have left weapons, fuel, scrap metal, and other resources to be salvaged by the Israelis. It seems more likely they will salvage figurative rather than actual wood, but it is hard to say. As the salvagers clear out the wreckage, they will set up markers as they find new bodies, so that those can be collected and buried as well. (See Ezekiel 39:15.)

It is this part of the prophecy—that the resources left by Gog's decimated army will be gathered for seven years—that made Tim LaHaye believe the latest this battle could be waged would be three and a half years before the beginning of the Tribulation, or seven years before the Abomination of Desolation and the beginning of the Great Tribulation, a time in which the Jewish population will be fleeing for their lives and will go into hiding. In other words, the seven-year burial and gathering period will overlap the first half of the Tribulation.

It also seems likely there would be a period of years before the Rapture—which I believe will happen just prior to the beginning of Daniel's Seventieth Week (and the beginning of the Tribulation)—allowing that *"This gospel of the kingdom shall be preached in the whole world as a testimony to all the nations, and then the end will come"* (Matthew 24:14). Israel will experience a time of relative peace again, in which God will work in their midst, returning His people to Himself, along with many others around the world.

*"And I will set My glory among the nations; and all the nations will see My judgment which I have executed and My hand which I have laid on them. And the house of Israel will know that I am the L*ORD *their God from that day onward. The nations will know that the house of Israel went into exile for their iniquity because they acted treacherously against Me, and I hid My face from them; so I gave them into the hand of their adversaries, and all of them fell by the sword. According to their uncleanness and according to their transgressions I dealt with them, and I hid My face from them."*

*Therefore thus says the Lord G*OD*, "Now I will restore the fortunes of Jacob and have mercy on the whole house of Israel; and I will be jealous for My holy name. They will forget their disgrace and all their treachery which they perpetrated against Me, when they live securely on their own land with no one to make them afraid. When I bring them back from the peoples and gather them from the lands of their enemies, then I shall be sanctified through them in the sight of the many nations. Then they will know that I am the L*ORD *their God because I made them go into exile among the nations, and then gathered them again to their own land; and I will leave none of them there any longer. I will not hide My face from them any longer, for I will have poured out My Spirit on the house of Israel," declares the Lord G*OD*.—Ezekiel 39:21-29*

THE RISE OF A WORLD GOVERNMENT

In the aftermath of this war, the influence of nations of Gog's coalition will be all but extinguished. In a world that is suddenly without Russia and the main financier of radical Shi'a Islam, Iran, the power blocks will become the West, China, and the Sunni nations of the Arabian Peninsula with the rejuvenated Iraq at its forefront. Al Qaeda has already fallen with the death of Bin Laden and will not likely rise again.

The world—likely through a body like the U.N.—will take a renewed interested in maintaining the peace of the Middle East because it was the host of this battle, and the most likely seat open for outside forces to make a home will be in Iraq. The rebuilding of Babylon could easily be the compromise to allow for this. As a sign to the world of their dedication to this aim, a united "world caliphate" will indeed rise out of the ashes of ancient Babylon, only it will not be a Shi'a messiah who initiates this unification. Instead it will be someone out of the last ruler seen in Daniel's vision of the statue. From the *"clay and iron"* remnants of the Roman Empire—the European Union—will arise a world leader who will seek to make the world one. He will unify all nations under one flag and all religions under the one all-encompassing Universalist doctrine. Today we can already see the forerunner in such teachings as the New Age and twisted metaphysics dogma.

It seems likely we will be around for at least part of the move to this, with the ultimate rise of this Antichrist. This acceptance of this counterfeit leader will be further facilitated by the final disappearance at the Rapture of all dissenting voices. For what will be left when the Church goes? The world is likely to see a huge shift to the political left, and the ultimate outcome of that cannot be pretty. The defeat of Gog's coalition will be an even more vivid sign of the coming of the last days than was the rebirth of the state of Israel. I truly believe it is the next great prophetic event, and as such, we need to be ready to act on God's behalf now, because once that happens, it will likely be too late to start.

NO PRIVATE INTERPRETATION

Before I close this chapter, I want to say that I am not a military analyst or expert on what needs to be done to invade or defend a country. My "imaginings" about what the attack of Gog might look like are formed only by what I have read of history, in the newspapers, and what comes to mind as I meditate on the Scriptures. What Ezekiel saw and described as *"arrows," "horses," "shield and buckler," "swords,"* and *"war clubs and spears"*—your guess is as good as mine. Did God give him a vision of these things in a way that he could understand in his own time, or did he look at men with machine guns riding in armored personnel carriers and describe them as a mounted cavalry? It is impossible to say. However, I feel it is valid to search these scriptures and see exactly how they might be fulfilled by examining what we do know.

Seeing how easily these prophecies could come about as things stand today adds one more set of signs that help determine the times in which we live. It is hard to look at these reports of earthquakes, a watering down of the Gospel among churches, false messiahs, and a Russo-Iranian alliance that sees itself called by Allah to wipe Israel from the face of the map, and not feel an urgency to be doing God's will every day without exception.

As I see it, there is no more time to wonder if Jesus is coming back soon. As these signs accelerate, if we don't start living like each day is our last day on Earth, we will miss the chance to act. When we see the signs of Matthew 24, it stresses all the more that we should be living the life of Matthew 25. The knowledge that Jesus is coming soon should not have us hoarding canned goods and heading for caves in the mountains to wait out His coming. It is a time to follow Him like those in the book of Acts did—a time to keep in step with the Holy Spirit as He works on the Earth for the final harvest of the Church Age. It is time to be the Christians we have always wanted to be, answering God's call and obeying as He speaks. If we do this, we face a very exciting time ahead!

Once again, these are not all the signs. If only these things were happening, there might be room for doubt; but there are other factors that indicate dramatic change is on the horizon. End-time prophecy also speaks of a monumental financial collapse that also may contribute to why Russia and its coalition attack Israel, or it may create a period of world war and unrest that will usher in the need for a one-world government to restore the peace. This will then pave the way for the leader (the Antichrist) who will come to power to end war and make a peace treaty with Israel that would last for seven years. On that day, the Tribulation will begin.

This economic chaos and the negotiated peace in Israel will be two other game changers that will mark the end of the Age. Will the actions of the Church be a third one? Certainly what God prophecies *will happen* whether we get involved or not, but we also have the potential to have an incredible impact in how these things affect individuals. Do we sit idly by and wait for Jesus to save us, or do we get involved through prayer and action just as Daniel did in his time? Do we choose to let the earth be "decimated" because so many are taken in the Rapture, or do we leave our neighbors to the wrath poured out in the Tribulation?

It is my conviction that we must act, and we must do what we can to help people weather the next two great crises: economic chaos and the outcome of negotiations between the Palestinians and Israelis. How likely are we to face such things? Where are we to stand? What forms are they likely to take? Are there already precursors happening in today's events? We will explore those questions in the next section.

PART FOUR:

Man is a strange animal. He generally cannot read the handwriting on the wall until his back is up against it.

—ADLAI STEVENSON

CHAPTER 10

THE DAY
THE DOLLAR DIES

When He broke the third seal, I heard the third living creature saying, "Come." I looked, and behold, a black horse; and he who sat on it had a pair of scales in his hand. And I heard something like a voice in the center of the four living creatures saying, "A quart of wheat for a denarius [day's wages], and three quarts of barley for a denarius; and do not damage the oil and the wine."

REVELATION 6:5-6 (INSERT ADDED)

If you study monetary history throughout thousands of years, you will find out that paper [fiat] money has been tried many, many times, and it never succeeds—it always ends badly. The question is: when will the dollar end badly? Will it be next year, or in five years, or in ten years? I am convinced it will end. —SENATOR RON PAUL

Interest in a turbulent period of history recently reemerged in the wake of the real estate bubble bursting in 2007 and 2008. The U.S.—followed by an avalanche of other countries—went into a recession that we are still struggling to escape, despite what the spin-masters in Washington are telling us. As a result, some have been reading up on post-World-War-I Germany under the Weimar Republic. This is the government that took over after the Kaiser was forced to step down, when Germany realized it could not win the war. It was this government that signed the Treaty of Versailles, accepting the famous "War-Guilt Clause." This treaty placed the responsibility for the war on Germany and made it promise to pay $33 billion in reparations—far more than its entire gold reserves.

As late as last summer, one of the rare books on the subject, *Dying of Money: Lessons of the Great German and American Inflations*, had a starting bid of $699 on EBay.[81] To answer this growing interest, another book written in the midst of the "stagflation" of the mid-1970s, *When Money Dies: The Nightmare of the Weimar Hyperinflation*, was reprinted because investors and politicians were paying as much as $1,800 for copies of the out-of-print title.[82]

The story of this period goes something like this: As World War I began, Germany decided to suspend the policy of converting its currency (called the Reichsbank mark at that time) into gold whenever its citizens asked to do so. This effectively severed the tie between the value of the mark and the price of gold and allowed the country to print more paper money, which they needed to finance the war.

The mark became what is known as a "fiat" currency: one whose value is backed by government promises rather than hard assets. The government reassured its public this was a solid policy, promising them, "A mark is a mark." In other words, nothing had really changed; it was still the same, stable currency it had always been. Even as government promises go, this would prove to be one of the all-time, great deceptions in world history.

The Kaiser's government decided that rather than raise taxes, it would borrow and print money to pay for its war efforts. This was a relatively new idea at the time; up to this point, most wars had been financed by raising taxes or selling war bonds. Printing new money and injecting it into the economy creates inflation, which is really a "back-door" tax: Instead of taking money out of peoples' pockets, it makes the money in their pockets decrease in value. As a result, the mark fell in value from about 4.2 marks to the dollar in 1913 to 8.91 marks to the dollar by the end of the war, halving its value. By the end of 1919, after the signing of the Treaty of Versailles,[83] it took 47 marks to buy a dollar. However, this was nothing compared to what would happen starting in June of 1921.

Faced with the huge war debt and backed by bad advice from economists, the Weimar government decided to increase the availability of money even further, one of the classic tactics still used today to stimulate an economy. Although it could not use this money to repay its war debts directly—the reparations had to be paid in a gold equivalent—the German government could pay its own bills to its citizens with this paper money. The thought was that the increased government spending would act as a catalyst to economic growth, prospering the country enough to repay its obligations less painfully and putting Germany back on the map as an economic power. At first, this seemed to be working.

Because the German population had gone into savings mode during the war, as the volume of available money increased, so did their savings. Salaries rose, and as a result people were willing to pay a little bit more for goods and services, allowing prices to increase. Inflation was relatively minor at first, and throughout the first half of 1921 the price of the dollar was about 60 marks. The first payment on the war debt was made in June of 1921, and since the economy was not growing quickly enough, more money was printed and put into circulation. This would prove to be the two-by-four that broke the camel's back.

Prices began to increase with the additional supply of money, and as they rose people dipped into their savings. Suddenly there was even more money in circulation. By November of 1921, the value of the mark had dropped to 330 marks to the dollar. Attempts to stabilize the currency were made by buying foreign exchange certificates with marks backed by treasury bills and commercial debt, but it didn't work. While the mark did stabilize until about the middle of 1922, hyperinflation kicked in when no other workable solution was implemented. By December of 1922, the mark fell to roughly 8,000 to the dollar. Consequently, Germany stopped paying on its war debt.

England and France accused Germany of destroying its economy to try to avoid paying what it owed. In January of 1923, in hopes of reclaiming some of the war debt, France and Belgian troops took over the industrial Ruhr region to collect revenues in goods and coal. German workers, however, refused to work for the occupying forces. To support their strikes, the German government continued to pay their salaries with freshly minted marks. It became a patriotic duty not to pay your taxes because German citizens were convinced that every mark they paid in taxes went straight to foreign countries.

You can imagine the hatred that was rising for the countries that were assumed to be plundering Germany while this was happening. In the next twelve months, the value of the mark went from roughly 18,000 marks to the dollar to *4.2 trillion* marks to the dollar. Inflation virtually halved the value of a mark *every month*. To give a physical example of how ridiculous this was, in October of 1923 it was noted by the British Embassy in Berlin that the exchange rate with the pound had reached the equivalent of the number of *yards* between the Earth and the sun.[84]

The German people began spending money as fast as possible because real goods held their value better than their currency did. There was little regard for the actual cost of goods, allowing prices to skyrocket. Marks literally lost their buying power by the minute. A barter system quickly came into play, and law and order broke down in the streets of major German cities. Pianos were traded for sacks of potatoes or sides of bacon. People would burn bundles of marks to heat their homes instead of using firewood because it cost more to buy the wood than the paper money was worth. Mobs descended on farms, convinced the farmers were hoarding food. They slaughtered animals on the spot, tearing the meat from the bones to take to their families. The price of a loaf of bread passed 1 billion marks.

The wealthy managed to grab hard assets or foreign currency to maintain their status, and many actually made money during this period. Those who could take out huge loans and buy costly machinery or make investments later had to pay back only minuscule amounts because by the time the payments came due, the currency was worth so much less. The working class organized strikes to demand wages to match the rate of inflation. The middle class, on the other hand—professionals, civil servants, landlords subject to rent controls on their properties, and those on fixed incomes, such as pensioners or those who lived from the interest thrown off by assets—became destitute. In a matter of months, the middle class evaporated. As a sense of panic and hopelessness set in, elderly couples gassed themselves in their apartments because they could not pay their bills or afford to buy food. Rather than face another day of despair, they chose to end their lives.

At the height of the crisis on November 9, 1923, a group of terrorists descended on a beer hall in Munich, where a local official was making a speech to a crowd of about 3,000. They declared they were going to take over the government and turn things around. The leader was eventually arrested and sentenced to five years in prison. His name was Adolf Hitler. Hitler would only serve one year of the sentence, but it was during that year that he wrote *Mein Kampf*, which made several references to the German war debt and its consequences.

Being imprisoned was a learning experience for the young man, who decided armed attempts to overthrow the government were fruitless. Instead, he became a politician. He whipped crowds of supporters into a frenzy by preying on their hatred and prejudices toward the U.S., Britain, and France primarily, blaming them for the imposed war debt that was causing Germany's suffering. Most historians agree that without the hyperinflation of the early 1920s, the seeds of the National Socialist German Worker's (Nazi) Party would never have taken root in the early 1930s.

Order was finally reinstated when the Retenmark—backed by bonds indexed to the market price of gold—was issued. It deleted twelve zeroes from the end of the former Reichsbank mark, and because it was tied to a hard commodity, it held its value. Within months a semblance of economic stability was restored. By this time the old marks became so worthless some actually used them to wallpaper rooms in their homes. Fifty-million mark notes became collectors' items, particularly in the United States.

Not willing to take the responsibility for the debacle, the government and media blamed bankers and speculators—many of whom were Jewish—for the rapid devaluation of their currency. The previously used Weimar Reichsbank marks came to be known by many as *Judefetzen*, or "Jew confetti." It was just one more resentment Hitler would use as a stepping-stone to being democratically elected roughly a decade later. As Adam Fergusson put it in the final lines of the introduction to *When Money Dies*:

> *This is, I believe, a moral tale. It goes far to prove the revolutionary axiom that if you wish to destroy a nation you must first corrupt its currency. Thus must sound money be the first bastion of a society's defense.*[85]

COULD IT HAPPEN AGAIN?

While you would be hard pressed to find an economist today who would say this could happen again, it is a period exactly like this that John is shown when the third seal is broken and the third Horseman of the Apocalypse is released:

> **When He broke the third seal, I heard the third living creature saying, "Come." I looked, and behold, a black horse; and he who sat on it had a pair of scales in his hand. And I heard something like a voice in the center of the four living creatures saying, "A quart of wheat for a denarius [a day's wages], and three quarts of barley for a denarius; and do not damage the oil and the wine."—Revelation 6:5-6**

Many agree that the scales in the hand of the rider of the black horse represent commerce, and that the pricing described in the next verse describes a time of great economic upheaval. A quart of wheat or three quarts of barley will go for a day's wages, while the price of things such as oil and wine will become their own units of value as bartered commodities. If we round the average annual salary today to $40,000, that would mean that a quart of wheat or three quarts of barley would cost $160. As inflation rises, however, that number would go up as well. John was seeing a time of economic chaos similar to the Weimar hyperinflation.

While 1923 Germany is not the only case of hyperinflation the world has ever experienced, it is one of the most startling and widely studied. Within a period of just a few months, everything fell apart. Although experts deny anything like it will ever happen again, it is interesting that those same experts are reading up on the Weimar hyperinflation with renewed vigor. Of course, these are also the same experts who told us the U.S. economy was strong and growing as late as the fall of 2007, before housing prices began to plummet in December.

Is there anything in recent history that could explain this fresh interest in the death of the Reichsbank mark? Unfortunately, I believe there is. I also believe the recent recession is just the tip of the iceberg. When the next bubble bursts—Internet, technology, real estate, credit, or whatever—what happened in Weimar Germany may well be the template for what happens with the world's most trusted currency of the last century: the U.S. dollar. With the huge bailouts of Wall Street investment banks and financial institutions in recent years, the instability caused by their massive risk-taking was simply transferred to our government.

In the meantime, Washington can't seem to figure out a way to reduce its own spending or take the hard course of raising revenues through biting the very hands that feed our economy. Could it be that we will face a situation where the dollar goes into such a nosedive in value that it will have to be replaced by another currency? And if it is replaced, how likely is it that it will be a one-world currency—the Euro, for instance—rather than a new U.S. currency?

What will happen to the U.S. if it is suddenly unable to repay its debts to China? Will the great People's Republic immediately want to seize chunks of the U.S., as happened with the Ruhr region—something like, say, the Alaskan oil fields—to recoup some of what is owed them?

Conspiracy theorizing? Doomsday thinking? Worst case scenario obsession? Again, I wish these thoughts and questions were so easily dismissed.

WHEN HISTORY REPEATS ITSELF

In July of 1944, as World War II still raged on, Allied representatives met at the Mount Washington Hotel in Bretton Woods, New Hampshire, to discuss what the world financial system should look like when the fighting was finally over. There were 730 delegates from forty-four nations in attendance. The delegates deliberated for three weeks. In that time they outlined the framework for the establishment of the International Monetary Fund (IMF) and the International Bank for Reconstruction and Development (IBRD), which are now part of the World Bank Group.

The foundation of the world currency would become the U.S. dollar, which would be exchanged directly for gold should the holder so desire, at an exchange rate of $35 an ounce. This would provide the foundation for the reconstruction of Europe after World War II, the prosperity of the 1950s and early 1960s, and would make the dollar the most important currency in the world. It added stability to the regulations imposed on the financial-services industry as a result of the Great Depression and led to a more than thirty-year period in which the United States did not experience a financial crisis.

However, in 1970, as the Vietnam War dragged on and spending by the federal government began to continually outstrip its income, the United States faced its first budget deficit since the end of World War II. From 1960, inflation had risen from 1.5 percent to 5 percent and unemployment had gone from 3.5 percent to 5 percent. These numbers might seem mild in today's climate, but at the time they seriously threatened Richard Nixon's reelection. To compensate for the growing imbalance and keep the economy moving, the Federal Reserve, which is the central bank of the United States, printed more money.

At the beginning of 1970, 55 percent of the dollars circulating in the world were backed by the gold in U.S. reserves. However, by the end of the year, that was reduced to 22 percent. In 1971, more money was printed to pay U.S. debts and a breaking point was being reached. West Germany, unwilling to let the mark devalue to prop up a weakening dollar, left the Bretton Woods agreement. France and Switzerland cashed in on the promise to redeem dollars for gold and significantly diminished U.S. gold holdings, causing a shift of financial stability from the United States to Europe.

Facing reelection in 1972, President Nixon needed a quick, bold fix for the rise in inflation and unemployment and the diminishing confidence in the dollar. Consequently, on August 15, 1971, he imposed a ninety-day wage and price freeze, introduced a 10 percent surcharge on all imports (newspeak for a "tariff"), and ended the promise to convert U.S. dollars into gold—unilaterally ending the Bretton Woods agreements once and for all.

At the time, the move looked like a stroke of genius. Decisive action won the hearts of the public, and the Dow-Jones Industrial Average (DJIA) jumped 32.9 points in one day, the largest one-day jump in the history of the stock market up to that point. The Federal Reserve ramped up the money printed—with no threat of inflation because of the price controls—and the economy responded. There was 10 percent more money available at the end of 1971 than there had been at the beginning, the biggest influx of new cash in U.S. history to that point. Nixon went on to win reelection in 1972 over George McGovern.

In the long-term, however, what came to be known as the "Nixon shock" proved to have been a bad idea. Gold quickly dropped to $44 per ounce, more than a 25-percent devaluation. This hit countries like Japan the hardest, because it had large dollar reserves. And a "floating" dollar paved the way to OPEC oil hikes in order to try to keep oil on a pace with the price of gold.

The controls implemented in August of 1971 had mostly been repealed by April of 1974 as complete failures, just four months before Nixon was forced to resign. The ninety-day freeze lasted three years. When it was removed, America saw double-digit inflation and the recession of 1974-1975. In 1977, Chrysler avoided bankruptcy only through a cash injection of government loans.

The promise to redeem dollars for gold was never restored. In fact, by March 1976 none of the major currencies of the world were tied to hard commodities any longer—all money was "floating" on government promises. By 1980 an ounce of gold was around $850, meaning the dollar was worth over twenty-four times *less* than what it had been worth a decade before, and the price of oil skyrocketed in an attempt to keep up.

It has been argued that the ability of the Federal Reserve to print— or literally to create out of thin air—more money in a crisis would keep the U.S. from another Great Depression. As evidence, many economists point to the more recent Black Monday of 1987 and to the current recession that occurred after the Wall Street bankruptcies of September 2008. The influx of cash from the Federal Reserve was designed to be a protection from "bank runs." When liquidity in banks dries up because their immediate obligations suddenly outweigh their liquid assets, the Federal Reserve comes to the rescue with cash "created" to keep the economy from falling off a cliff. Thus the Federal Reserve becomes the "lender of last resort," "loaning" money to institutions to which no other entity in the market is willing to loan money. And, of course, this is money that didn't exist before it was loaned out.

STIMULATING A FLAGGING ECONOMY

Making more money available—as is also done when interest rates are dropped, more money is printed, or the ratio of bank holdings to loans is allowed to increase—acts to stimulate an economy because it increases spending. On the other hand, when the central bank raises interest rates or buys back treasury bonds and takes money out of circulation, it slows the economy and pushes it towards deflation, a rather negative term despite the fact that it means an increase in the value of a currency.

In some ways, it is like simple supply and demand: When more money is available, there is more money for everyone to earn and spend, increasing its exchange; but it also gradually loses value because more of it exists. If this is managed well for an extended period of time, this can look like the economic growth the U.S. experienced in the 1990s and early 2000s, while Alan Greenspan was chairman of the Federal Reserve. However, economies can't defy gravity forever—what goes up still must come down at some point, and more often than not, it comes crashing down.

If you look at recent news, you will see many credit Ben Bernanke and the Federal Reserve with keeping the crisis of 2008 from turning into a full-blown depression. You don't have to dig too much deeper, however, to discover that not everyone agrees with that assessment. Every U.S. dollar had to be backed by gold in a vault somewhere until 1933, when we went off an absolute gold standard. From 1933 until 2008, the Federal Reserve had "created" only about 800 billion dollars, a number that included the quantities that shook things up in the early 1970s. In the months following the bankruptcy of Lehman Brothers on September 15, 2008, the Federal Reserve got on the phone and purchased $1.25 trillion in toxic assets—roughly one-fifth of the mortgage-backed securities in the United States—all with money that didn't exist before the transactions were completed.

In the fifteen months following the bankruptcy of Lehman Brothers, the Federal Reserve created a total of $2.4 trillion in programs like this by printing more money.[86] This is completely separate from 1) the trillions borrowed by Congress to bail out AIG, Goldman Sachs, Chrysler, GM, and others; 2) the TARP funds; and 3) the Bush and Obama stimulus packages. While the debates over these things were going on in Congress and dominating the nightly news, the Fed was creating incredible sums of money that dwarfed those plans without anyone really batting an eyelash.

At present, this "new" money mostly sits on the bank balance sheets—much like the savings of German citizens after World War I. As Ron Paul describes it in his book, *End the Fed*:

> This new money now sits as reserves in bank
> vaults awaiting a safe environment for lending and

borrowing. Should that environment arrive, we would see a level of price increases none of us has experienced in our lifetime.

Some people think the experience of the Weimar Republic in Germany in the interwar years, when paper money was made so worthless by the central bank that the bills were literally used as fuel to heat homes, is entirely impossible in the United States.

We think we are immune from such a calamity, but we are not.

Bad economic policy can destroy a civilization—no policy is more dangerous than bad monetary policy.

The fact that the Fed can create trillions of dollars and distribute them to its cronies without congressional oversight should shock us all.[87]

An economic time bomb of inflation is ticking, and it's close to zero-hour. Whether or not this will turn into what John described in Revelation 6:5-6, I can't say, but it certainly could. If it isn't defused, the next financial crisis will have unprecedented ramifications, and right now everyone in government seems convinced that a Great Depression could never happen again. Of course, these are the same people who said over and over in 2007 that housing prices would only go up and that the economy was too strong to go into recession. We have only begun to see how that has turned out.

Those who look beyond the glossy surface hold Alan Greenspan and the Federal Reserve responsible for creating the problem in the first place. Keeping interest rates low for too long fed the monster of Wall Street with cheap credit that was used for greater leverage to invest with all the more risk. This very thing caused the housing bubble to grow out of proportion. Greenspan seems to have been a genius in keeping the equilibrium for so long, but eventually someone is going to have to pay for our dinner, and all he did was make sure he was long gone when the waitress came looking for him with the check. The long-term effects of his policies and deregulation fed the bubble that caused the Wall Street bankruptcies and made the bailouts of 2008 necessary—if they didn't, in fact, create them in the first place.

THEN AND NOW

In 1971, before the "Nixon shock," an ounce of gold could be exchanged for $35. In recent months (fall of 2011), the price of an ounce of gold has surpassed $1,800. In 1971, the price of a barrel of oil was around $3.60 (worth a little more than a tenth of an ounce of gold) and a gallon of regular gas was around 36 cents. A typical new home would run you less than $30,000, and the median household income was $9,028.

Paul Volker, who became the chairman of the Federal Reserve under Jimmy Carter and was reappointed by Ronald Reagan, said that his Wall Street salary as vice president and director of planning for Chase Manhattan Bank was in the neighborhood of $45,000 when he left to be the undersecretary of the Treasury in 1969. And that was a very good living.

In 2011, the price of oil was closing in on $120 a barrel (about .07 ounces of gold, using round estimates), the price of a gallon of gas flirted with $4.00, and the average price of a home was $246,800, even after the housing bubble "corrected." The National Average Wage Index (last updated in 2009) puts the present average wage at $40,711.61.[88] The annual compensation package for a vice president at an investment bank is around $245,000, and a managing director takes home somewhere between $400,000 and tens of millions of dollars each year.[89] While normal salaries have increased fourfold, investment bankers' salaries have increased five to tenfold, if not more.

In 1982 the top 1 percent of America's wealthiest individuals held about 10 percent of U.S. wealth; in 2006 they had about 23 percent of it. From 1980 to 2006, the portion of the top 10 percent of American's wealthiest went from 35 percent to 49 percent. The present generation graduating from college is the first in American history to look forward to a lower standard of living than their parents had at that age.

Upward mobility, the core of the American dream, has changed as well. The entrance to the American dream, a college education, has gone from a gateway to opportunities to a virtual debtors' prison. Now, when parents receive financial aid packages, loans are part of the "aid." Tuition for a term in a state college in California was $650 in 1977; in 2009 it was over $10,000. Things have certainly changed, and not for the better.

Of course, there are many factors that have gone into these figures besides the dollar going off a gold standard. For one, in 1970 the U.S. still provided much of its own oil and natural gas. OPEC was in its first decade, and the oil embargo caused by U.S. support of Israel in the Yom Kippur War was still ahead. The OPEC oil embargo would increase oil prices tenfold. Then Islamic Revolution of 1979 in Iran sent oil prices up tenfold, increasing oil revenues a hundredfold in less than a decade. However, it is interesting to note that the price of oil in gold today is more than 20 percent *less*—more than one-fifth less—than it was forty years ago.

What would have happened had Bretton Woods never been negated or the Federal Reserve had never been given the ability to print dollars without solid assets behind them? Some argue that the increase of wars in the nineteenth and twentieth centuries was a direct result of central banks being able to print money to pay for them just as Germany did in 1913. The U.S. did a very similar thing to enter World War I. It is quite possible that *"wars and rumors of wars"* are a direct result of nations being able to pay their bills by printing money without the check of having to finance them more responsibly. Fiscal irresponsibility literally makes waging war easier.

Is the dollar in danger of going the way of the Reichsbank mark? While that is very difficult to say with much certainty, since the crisis of 2008 people are asking this question more than they have in many years.

As I write this the government and media are repeatedly telling us that things are getting back to normal. The economy is growing again. Raising the debt ceiling for government spending is a stopgap measure. They will get government spending under control. And most importantly, Wall Street has learned from its mistakes. However, early 2000's "business as usual" is simply the recipe for guaranteed disaster at some point down the road.

The economy is always stimulated when there is a lot of spending, which is happening right now, but how long can that last? What will happen to the value of the dollar when all the "new" money the Fed recently created starts going into circulation? Will we then see the hyperinflation described in Revelation 6:5-6?

Have we truly learned our lesson? Are we really out of the woods of the 2008 recession? Where are the necessary safeguards to keep us from another financial crisis in the next decade? And what will happen to the dollar and America when the next economic bubble bursts?

Economic experts say that unless things change quickly, there will be another bubble; and when there is, we're not going to be able to spend our way out of it. Is that where we are headed?

CHAPTER 11

DIVIDING
JERUSALEM

*"Behold, I am going to make Jerusalem a cup that causes
reeling to all the peoples around. . . . It will come about
in that day that I will make Jerusalem a heavy stone for
all the peoples; all who lift it will be severely injured. And
all the nations of the earth will be gathered against it."*

ZECHARIAH 12:2-3

The United States believes that negotiations
should result in two states, with permanent Palestinian
borders with Israel, Jordan, and Egypt, and permanent
Israeli borders with Palestine. The borders of Israel
and Palestine should be based on the 1967 lines with
mutually agreed swaps, so that secure and recognized
borders are established for both states.

Two wrenching and emotional issues remain:
the future of Jerusalem, and the fate of Palestinian
refugees.

—BARAK OBAMA

Speech given at the State Department,
May 19, 2011

Jerusalem is not a settlement. It is our capital.

— BENJAMIN NETANYAHU
Address at AIPAC
March 23, 2010

As his presidency was coming to a close, Bill Clinton made a last, desperate attempt to be remembered for more than his impeachment and the Monica Lewinski scandal. He wanted to be the man who finally brought a solution to the Israeli-Palestinian conflict. It was the boldest and most expansive offer to the Palestinians yet. According to Arab sources, the offer to the PLO was 98 percent of Judea, Samaria, and Gaza, all of East Jerusalem except the Jewish and Armenian quarters, sovereignty over the Temple Mount—with the concession that Jews could still pray at the Western Wall—and a fund of $30 billion to jump start a Palestinian infrastructure. This plan used the 1967 borders as the starting point and worked from there, conceding primarily the rights of the Jews to access their beloved portions of East Jerusalem and settlements in that immediate area. In laying the plan before Arafat at Camp David, Clinton told him, "It's five minutes to midnight, Mr. Chairman, and you are about to lose the only opportunity that your people will ever get to solve their problem on satisfactory ground by not being able to make a decision. . . . The Israelis accepted."[90]

However, Arafat had a different take. It was not enough. There would be no "sharing" the holy places. As far as he was concerned, these areas had always been sacred Arab places. Furthermore, as a vice president of the Arab council (the Arab council had many vice presidents at that time), he could not accept allowing Jews into East Jerusalem to pray at the foot of the mount that was home to the Dome of the Rock and the al-Aqsa Mosque. Arafat turned the offer down.

According to Danny Ayalon, the present deputy foreign minister for Israel, Prime Minister Ehud Barak told him that even President Clinton was shocked by Yasser Arafat's proclamation, and the president grew red in the face. Mr. Ayalon said:

> *Clinton, flabbergasted by Arafat's rejection, told him, "Mr. Arafat, are you telling me that all my history is wrong? That my Bible is wrong? That my faith is wrong? So let me tell you: 2,000 years ago, when Jesus walked this land here, and visited these holy places, He didn't see even one mosque, only synagogues."*[91]

But it was to no avail. There was no reasoning with him. The PLO had no interest in an agreement that gave the Palestinians a homeland with enough room for them to live comfortably, even with *most of* East Jerusalem as a capital. It was all or nothing.

The possession of Jerusalem was then—as it is now—a stumbling block.

At the time, much of Washington and the rest of the United States were floored by how much of Israel Clinton was willing to give away in order to redeem his presidency for the history books. The concessions he was able to illicit from Prime Minister Barak and his government were astonishing, but Clinton almost succeeded. When Arafat rejected the proposed agreement, Americans and Arabs alike were shocked that such a monumental opportunity for Palestinian victory had been turned down. It was the chance of a lifetime, and refusing it would doom the Palestinians for at least a generation . . . or so many thought.

It would not be a generation but only the passing of two terms of a Republican president. It appears from President Obama's activities since taking office that he wants to pick up and move forward from where Clinton left off. All it would take for Israel to be sold out again is for the White House to be back into the hands of a liberal Democrat who, though he claims to be a Christian, seems to have little allegiance to a Bible that repeatedly warns not to divide the land of Israel.

We stand at a critical stage. In May 2011 President Obama and Prime Minister Netanyahu exchanged expectations of one another in a series of speeches before the State Department, The American Israeli Public Affairs Committee (AIPAC), and the U.S. Congress. Obama had let it leak to reporters that the White House didn't have confidence that Netanyahu had the political clout to make the tough concessions that would pave the way for a treaty with the Palestinians. That same week, Netanyahu exchanged angry words with Secretary of State Hilary Clinton when he discovered Obama would call for a return to pre-1967 borders for a future Palestinian state.

Meanwhile, the Palestinian Authority presented its petition to the United Nations for unilaterally recognizing a Palestinian state on September 23, 2011 *without* a negotiated settlement and in violation of the Oslo Accords of the early 1990s. Obama had promised to veto such a resolution, but will America sit by and let other allies vote to upgrade Palestine to observer status in the General Assembly in what would be an unsettling statement of world opinion? Is the United States willing to quietly stand by and let the world paint Israel into a corner it may have no choice but to fight its way out of?

All this posturing might seem like political gymnastics if it weren't for two things: 1) The Bible tells us God will judge the people and nations who divide the land of Israel:

> *For behold, in those days and at that time* [in the latter days], *When I restore the fortunes of Judah and Jerusalem, I will gather all the nations And bring them down to the valley of Jehoshaphat. Then I will enter into judgment with them there On behalf of My people and My inheritance, Israel, Whom they have scattered among the nations; And they have divided up My land.—Joel 3:1-2* [insert and emphasis added]

And 2) One day the Antichrist will cut a covenant of peace with Israel that will mark the beginning of the Tribulation—Daniel's Seventieth Week. As we discussed earlier, Daniel foresaw:

> *"He* [the Antichrist] *will make a firm covenant with the many* [Israel and other nations] *for one week, but in the middle of the week he will put a stop to sacrifice and grain offering; and on the wing of abominations will come one who makes desolate* [the Abomination of Desecration], *even until a complete destruction, one that is decreed, is poured out on the one who makes desolate."*—Daniel 9:27 [inserts added]

While there is no indication that these two scriptures should be taken as representing the same event, it is interesting that both seem to describe exactly what is on the table for Israel and Palestine today—namely land for peace, or dividing Israel and Jerusalem for the promise of peace and security—perhaps the same peace and security we read about in Ezekiel 38.

It is interesting that the angel speaking to Daniel didn't just describe it as a covenant, but he called it *"a firm* covenant" (emphasis added). Could it be that this is not a treaty that is mutually agreed upon, but one that is hard on Israel—even perhaps one that is *forced* on Israel? A unilateral recognition of a Palestinian state in Judea and Samaria by the Quartet (The U.N., U.S., E.U., and Russia), forcing Israel to concede land without believing the new borders are defensible, would indeed be a "firm" or difficult agreement. There would have to be a very active and involved "peace-keeping" force of outside nations in Israel to keep such a treaty from turning into open war.

Many scoff when they hear of end-time prophecies and the return of Jesus Christ. They believe such is the domain of extremists, especially considering the recent, widely publicized prediction that He would return on May 21, 2011. However, they don't realize just how incredible it is that over 2,500 years ago the Bible prophets predicted Israel would be reborn as a nation, would be under constant duress from its neighbors—particularly Russia and Iran—and that the Land would be a topic of continual discussion. Despite counterfeit signs and mistaken interpretations, the Scriptures do, in fact, point to events just as they are playing out today.

Regardless of President Obama's unwillingness to stand solidly on the side of the strongest U.S. ally in the Middle East if not the world, his frank announcement that "The United States believes that negotiations should result in two states . . . based on the 1967 lines with mutually agreed swaps," should be the stance that shocks us the most. Is it really a given that the U.S. believes that a two-state solution is the only option? Can the Palestinians win simply by refusing to give an inch in negotiations time after time—even though they align with those who openly commit acts of terror and refuse to acknowledge Israel's right to exist?

From a worldly perspective, perhaps a two-state solution seems politically expedient. However, from a biblical perspective, if we are part of a coalition of nations that forces the division of Jerusalem and the nation of Israel as the compromise that will bring "peace and security" to the Middle East, then we are not only fooling ourselves but also aligning ourselves with the nations that will be judged when Jesus returns. There is no plausible deniability in Heaven's courtroom! Even if we simply acquiesce by stepping aside and putting the burden of decision upon the U.N., we are complicit in standing against God's people.

There is no salvation in sitting on the fence. What is right and just is not decided democratically. Justice must be decided objectively by the rule of law. That is why courts have judges who decide cases based on law and precedent, not committee members who base decisions on the feedback of opinion polls and focus groups. Though I wish I could, I cannot say that Israel has never erred in relating to the Palestinians, but I can say it has been governed by law and has done everything it can to guard the human rights of the Palestinians as well as others within their borders.

Israel's military does everything it can short of letting criminals escape to protect civilians. Just as Goldstone eventually rejected the condemnations in his report that accused Israel of retaliating without conscience, its leaders do everything to react as humanely as possible, targeting criminals and terrorists rather than choosing public places and civilian gatherings as targets. Yet somehow this criticism is never leveled against groups who indiscriminately shoot rockets into Israeli villages and hide behind hospitals and daycare centers as they do it.

Where does America truly stand on this issue today? How close are we to a two-state "solution" to the Israeli-Palestinian conflict? Will the next treaty with Israel be the one that starts the Tribulation or, as Tim LaHaye suggests in *The Coming Peace in the Middle East,* simply the precursor to the attack of Gog's coalition—the next tick on God's prophetic countdown?

WHEELING AND DEALING IN THE MIDDLE EAST

Soon after his inauguration President Obama sent Special Envoy Richard Holbrooke to Saudi Arabia in hopes of obtaining the king's help in getting U.S. troops out of Afghanistan. He urged Saudi Arabia to use its influence to end support for the Taliban and Al-Qaeda in Afghanistan and Pakistan. He worked to secure Israel's flyover rights should military action be needed to halt Iran's nuclear threat—something the Saudis have no more desire to happen than Israel does. Although the Arabian Peninsula would not be Iran's first target, they are not friends with Iran.

Sensing the opportunity to use these requests as leverage, King

Abdullah agreed to help on the condition that the United States support the Saudi plan to divide Israel into two nations, using the pre-1967 borders as the new national boundaries. According to one news source:

> *Diplomatic sources said Obama relayed a pledge to Saudi King Abdullah that he would take any measure to ensure an Israeli withdrawal from the West Bank and Jerusalem over the next 18 months. They said Obama relayed the pledge to Abdullah during the president's trip to Riyadh in June 2009, about four months after he assumed office, in exchange for Abdullah's help to arrange for the end of the Taliban war in Afghanistan.*[92]

During his initial visit with the king in April of 2009, the president bowed to the Saudi monarch, an unprecedented act of subservience for a U.S. head of state. Obama seems to literally be bowing to Arab wishes in general, in order to solve what he announced as the top two most pressing "tensions" in the world today: 1) "violent extremism in all of its forms," and 2) "the situation between Israelis, Palestinians, and the Arab world."[93]

Oddly enough, in a seemingly unrelated set of circumstances, in August of 2009 Palestinian Prime Minister Salam Fayyad published a report called, "Palestine: Ending the Occupation, Establishing the State."[94] On the surface the report appears to outline a plan for the Palestinian Authority to develop the infrastructure it would need to govern itself at some point in the future. This would all be done on a two-year timetable.

Initially it was reported that Israeli officials received the plan positively because it suggested the PA would build governmental institutions and improve its own internal security services. However, other sources reported there was another part of the plan that was being kept secret: the call for unilateral recognition of a state of Palestine outlined by 1967 borders, with East Jerusalem as its capital. According to one article:

Fayyad is also seeking a new Security Council resolution to replace Resolutions 242 and 338 in the hope of winning the international community's support for the borders of a Palestinian state and applying stronger pressure on Israel to withdraw from the West Bank.

Several Israeli officials told Haaretz that Fayyad had spoken to them of positive responses he had received over the plan from prominent E.U. member states, including the United Kingdom, France, Spain, and Sweden. Fayyad added that he presented the proposal to the U.S. administration and did not receive any signal of opposition in response.[95]

Odd, isn't it, that this two-year period ends almost exactly at the time Abbas presented his petition for the unilateral recognition of Palestine as a state to the U.N. General Assembly? In the meantime, Washington has stalled or denied almost every request from Israel's leaders for the weapons needed to keep ahead of their hostile neighbors.

On September 2, 2010, Israeli Prime Minister Netanyahu and Palestinian President Mahmoud Abbas met with Secretary of State Clinton and President Obama in Washington for a peace summit. It was the first meeting between Netanyahu and Abbas in twenty months. Prime Minister Netanyahu greeted the Palestinian President with hopeful words:

> *"I see in you a partner for peace. Together we can lead our people to a historic future that can put an end to claims and to conflict. Now this will not be easy. A true peace, a lasting peace would be achieved only with mutual and painful concessions from both sides."*[96]

Despite the goodwill, negotiations that were to outline a one-year interim agreement again broke down before they were even begun. Only days later on September 7, Abbas revealed his true feelings in an interview with *Al-Quds*:

> *We're not talking about a Jewish state and we won't talk about one. For us, there is the state of Israel and we won't recognize Israel as a Jewish state.*[97]

In April of 2011, the Palestinian Authority buried its past differences and rivalries with HAMAS and made plans for a joint government. With HAMAS openly refusing to recognize the right of Israel to exist, it seemed obvious the PA had no plans of returning to the negotiating table with Israel anytime soon. It seems to not only be holding out for the U.N. vote in September but also preparing for it by accepting the old axiom that "the enemy of my enemy is my friend."

Despite the lack of negotiations, somehow it still felt like Obama's and the PA's timeline of having a Palestinian state by September of 2011 had marched on. As we have already discussed, Mr. Netanyahu came to Washington in May of 2011 to try to strengthen ties with the United States. However, Obama gave him a chilly reception, and it was even leaked to the press: "President Obama has told aides and allies that he does not believe that Mr. Netanyahu will ever be willing to make the kind of big concessions that will lead to a peace deal."[98]

Artfully preempting Mr. Netanyahu's speech to Congress, which would take place on May 24, Obama addressed the State Department on May 19, putting forth his "belief" about a two-state solution based on the 1967 borders "with mutually agreed swaps." It was a shot across the bow of the Israeli ship of state, one that hinted at a direction and stance but would still leave the White House a good deal of maneuvering room. It was a broad outline within which the U.N. would have to hammer out the details. This appears to be another important international policy decision where President Obama is willing to let the U.S. be a follower rather than a leader in keeping its allies and the world safe.

Meanwhile, when Mr. Netanyahu spoke to Congress on the 24th, he was received with numerous standing ovations. The speech was obviously designed to warm the icy relations with the White House and win the hearts of Americans everywhere. At the same time, he boldly announced that Israel would not let East Jerusalem be turned into another Gaza that could be targeted with rockets. While he said Israel was committed to a two-state solution, Mr. Netanyahu cautioned:

> The vast majority of the 650,000 Israelis who live beyond the 1967 lines reside in neighborhoods and suburbs of Jerusalem and Greater Tel Aviv.
>
> These areas are densely populated but geographically quite small. Under any realistic peace agreement, these areas, as well as other places of critical strategic and national importance, will be incorporated into the final borders of Israel.
>
> The status of the settlements will be decided only in negotiations. But we must also be honest. So I am saying today something that should be said publicly by anyone serious about peace. In any peace agreement that ends the conflict, some settlements will end up beyond Israel's borders. The precise delineation of those borders must be negotiated. We will be very generous on the size of a future Palestinian state. But as President Obama said, the border will be different than the one that existed on June 4, 1967. Israel will not return to the indefensible lines of 1967.[99]

Thus, the future of Jerusalem is once again at the center of the conflict.

As I write this, we face two major issues: 1) The Palestinian government will not acknowledge the right of Israel to exist as a Jewish state, and 2) The occupation and authority over Jerusalem and the Temple Mount is in dispute. If rebuilding the Temple as Daniel and Ezekiel saw is part of the Antichrist's peace agreement, then that is not likely to change too much in the years to come. It could well be that the disposition of the Temple Mount will be a key component of Israel's future covenant with the Antichrist.

THE CITY AT THE CENTER OF PROPHECY

In their book, *Jerusalem, Song of Songs*, Jill and Leon Uris described this city of dispute in this way:

> Jerusalem has known the hosts of thirty-six wars. She has been reduced to ashes seventeen times. She has risen eighteen. She has been sanctified by blood and martyrdom. She knew the hoof beat of Assyrian war chariots, chilled to the besieging battering machines of Rome, heard the hissing arcs of Saladin's sabers, and the rattle of crusader mail . . . and the tattoo of Israeli paratroop gunfire. She has seen more passion and love and more human savagery than any other place in the world.
>
> Jerusalem has variously been described as the center of the world, the eye of the world, and the navel of the world. She is regarded as the halfway house between heaven and earth. . . . Jerusalem is

the greatest of the great, for she alone has achieved immortality on moral and ethical grounds.[100]

Scripture does not tell us to pray for the peace of Israel but to *"pray for the peace of Jerusalem"* (Psalm 122:6). This is the city that is the apple of God's eye and where Jesus will come to live and rule after His return to Earth.

Where the United States stands in regard to Jerusalem is very likely to be the side on which it stands in the Tribulation, if it exists at that time.[101] However, we have been given instructions in God's Word and have a responsibility to carry them out. Even if the Church is not here during the Tribulation and Daniel's Seventieth Week, until the day we meet the Lord in the air we must stand with an Israel that recognizes Jerusalem as its capital.

The only way the city of Jerusalem will know peace in our time is if we fervently pray for her.[102]

CHAPTER 12

THE CHURCH'S
FINEST HOUR

*"Who then is the faithful and sensible slave whom his
master put in charge of his household to give them their
food at the proper time? Blessed is that slave whom his
master finds so doing when he comes."*

MATTHEW 24:45-46

So often when I discuss Bible prophecies and how they
are being reflected in the events of our times, one of the first questions
always seems to be, "So what are we supposed to do? How do we prepare
ourselves? If things are going to just get worse and worse, what can we
possibly do?"

I believe the answers to such questions are in the Bible, and very
often in the same passages of Scripture that tell us how things will be
in the latter days. It seems very few realize that the Olivet Discourse so
often quoted concerning end-time events (Matthew 24) is only partially
about signs of the final days. In fact, the signs of the end of the age
are only discussed in the first third of that sermon, which encompasses
Matthew 24-25.

The other two thirds is comprised of four parables:

> »   The Parable of the Faithful Servant (Matthew 24:45-51)

> »   The Parable of the Ten Virgins (Matthew 25:1-13)

» The Parable of the Talents (Matthew 25:14-30)

» The Parable of the Sheep and the Goats (Matthew 25:31-46)

Finally, Jesus closed His sermon declaring that in only a few days, He would be delivered for sacrifice on the Cross:

> *"You know that after two days the Passover is coming, and the Son of Man is to be handed over for crucifixion." —Matthew 26:2*

Why did He tell them He was about to be crucified at this time, and why did He use the signs of the last days as an introduction to these parables? For the answers, let's look at the basic structure of each of the parables:

» The servant's master goes away and leaves him in charge of the household, and there is a blessing for the servant if all has been well cared for when the master returns.

» The ten virgins wait vigilantly for the coming of the bridegroom.

» *"For it is just like a man about to go on a journey"* (Matthew 25:14).

» *"When the Son of Man comes in His glory"* (Matthew 25:31).

Every one of these parables is about what to do *while the master is away*. They are an outline of the responsibilities of believers while Jesus is in Heaven during the Church Age. Oddly enough, not one of them is about building a bomb shelter and stocking it with food or selling all possessions to go up onto a mountaintop to wait. Nor are any of them about putting on large campaigns declaring the date and time Jesus will return. In fact, they seem to depict just the opposite.

What these parables do discuss is the danger of going through the day-to-day motions of life living for your own plans and desires, ignoring the signs, and risking getting caught unprepared by the *"thief in the night"* (Matthew 24:43). Jesus said (my paraphrase): "These are the signs of My return. These are the things you are to do while I am gone. I am leaving in just a couple of days, and I need you to know these things so that you know what to do until I return."

According to Matthew's gospel, this was the final sermon Jesus shared with His disciples before the Last Supper. It is worth looking at more closely in this context in order to see what He emphasized to His followers, which includes you and me.

THE GREATEST SERMON EVER GIVEN . . .PART TWO

Just as Daniel read Jeremiah and knew the remaining days of Israel's exile were numbered, so we can look at the signs Jesus and the prophets gave us and know we are in the season of His return. While many have looked at their own time in history and observed some of the signs of the end of the age, we are living in a time when *all* of the signs are coming together in mounting intensity. Without a doubt Israel, the fig tree, has come to life, and *"its branch has already become tender and puts forth its leaves"* (Matthew 24:32). The spirit of antichrist is thriving and spreading. The Earth is groaning with earthquakes, tornadoes, hurricanes, and other natural disasters—waiting for the manifestation of the sons and daughters of God to rule it in righteousness rather than the corruption it is now experiencing through sin. It is literally convulsing with birth pangs for a new age to be born.

Knowledge and ease of travel are increasing as never before and will continue to do so at an accelerating pace. Persecution, slavery, terrorism, famine, poverty, sickness, and crime plague millions, many of them innocent children. Yet while this darkness grows, a revival of immense proportion is shaking the world afresh. The Church Age that started in Jerusalem is coming full-circle and is returning there again. Churches are sprouting up in Israel and throughout the Middle East. Meanwhile, Persia rattles its saber, threatening a war that could very well be the breaking of the first and second seals of Revelation 6:

> *Then I saw when the Lamb broke one of the seven seals, and I heard one of the four living creatures saying as with a voice of thunder, "Come." I looked, and behold, a white horse, and he who sat on it had a bow; and a crown was given to him, and he went out conquering and to conquer.*
>
> *When He broke the second seal, I heard the second living creature saying, "Come." And another, a red horse, went out; and to him who sat on it, it was granted to take peace from the earth, and that men would slay one another; and a great sword was given to him.—Revelation 6:1-4*

Just as Daniel looked into the book of Jeremiah and calculated the end of an age, we can see in the prophecies of Jesus, the apostles, and the Old Testament prophets that we are nearing the end of an age ourselves. To this realization, Jesus poses the question:

> *"Who then is the faithful and wise servant, whom his master has set over his household, to give them their food at the proper time? Blessed is that servant whom his master will find so doing when he comes. Truly, I say to you, he will set him over all his possessions."—Matthew 24:45-47* ESV

Just as a master leaves instructions for his household as he prepares for a long journey, Jesus left these instructions to us when He returned to Heaven:

> *"All authority has been given to Me in heaven and on earth. Go therefore and make disciples of all the nations, baptizing them in the name of the Father and the Son and the Holy Spirit, teaching them to observe all that I commanded you; and lo, I am with you always, even to the end of the age."—Matthew 28:18-20*

Jesus didn't say to go out into the world and make *converts*; He said to go out into the world and make *disciples*. For three years He had been teaching them what a disciple was. It was someone who could hear from Heaven, take divine instructions, and go in His power and authority to administer God's saving grace to others—spirit, soul, and body. It was not just someone who knew how to pray the prayer of salvation, but someone who could also petition for wisdom and intercede for others. It was not just someone who could renew their own spirits, but someone who had an overflow of the Spirit to significantly contribute to society and make a difference in the lives of the people around them.

Disciples are not just ministers and evangelists; they are teachers, businesspeople, inventors, workers, and leaders. Disciples are innovators, people of positive change that reflects their day-to-day integrity. They are the ones who bring restoration from corruption. They are the voice of moral clarity in a world blinded by selfish ambition and greed. It is their mission to confront an upside-down world and set it aright.

Before science was stolen from Christianity by an atheistic interpretation of evolution, the domain of invention and the application of natural law for the betterment of humanity was the realm of the disciples of Jesus. Newton's greatest work was not just the discovery of the law of gravity but his written commentary on the Bible. He spent more time studying it than anything else. Galileo was a courageous Christian who clashed with the hypocritical church of his day. And men such as George Washington Carver walked in a faith that unlocked the mysteries of creation and helped others. The simple peanut was thrown away as trash until Carver found over three hundred new uses for it through prayer and study.

William Wilberforce and those of the Clapham community used their influence and political power to end slavery and institute many other significant reforms for society in the British Commonwealth. Moreover, institutions such as unemployment offices, health and safety inspections in factories, and occupational retraining for laborers who had lost their jobs were first inspired not by a political party or government but by the work of the Salvation Army. To paraphrase Marley's ghost from *A Christmas Carol:* As Christians, humanity is our business. The common welfare is our business; charity, mercy, forbearance, and benevolence, are, all, our business. The dealings of our work and trade are but a drop of water in the comprehensive ocean of our business!

In a sense, every experiment of God upon the Earth has failed to this point because we human beings have not upheld our end. Ever since mankind was driven from the Garden of Eden because Adam and Eve sinned, God has reached out to humanity through His covenant people. Each generation of believers in Him has had its triumphs and defeats, some bringing nations to God while others were destroyed in their corruption, lust, and greed. Now it is the Church to which He has given His authority and wisdom to reach a lost world. I can't say our track record has been all that great. As we enter what could be the final lap, we should not view our time as a time of tragedy and destruction but one filled with the greatest potential for the expansion of the kingdom of God the world has never known!

In the end God will redeem the entire Earth and all who love Him, but those willing and obedient will have a major part in the manifestation of that redemption. In the days before the Tribulation, God will see the Church become all she was meant to be *before* she is raptured. The message of the Gospel will reach every people group on the Earth, and the Word of God will be presented to everyone. Bible translators actually estimate that the Bible will be translated into every dialect and language on Earth in the next decade-and-a-half, if not sooner. Then the Church will be taken out, and it will be time for the salvation of Israel to be worked out during the Tribulation. At the end of that epoch, Jesus will return for His millennial reign upon an Earth which will once again be the Eden God designed.

In the meantime, we are the servants who have been left in charge of the house while the Master is away. How are we doing in taking care of things? Are we attending to our true business, or are we distracted by the riches, pleasures, and cares of this world? The question reminds me of one of the final scenes in the movie *Schindler's List*. As the war ends and Oscar Schindler contemplates his riches and the lives he has saved with his wealth, he laments,

> *This car. Goeth would have bought this car. Why did I keep the car? Ten people right there. Ten people. Ten more people. [Removing a Nazi pin from his lapel.] This pin. Two people. This is gold. Two more people. He would have given me two for it, at least one. One more person. A person, Stern. For this. [Sobbing.] I could have gotten one more person . . . and I didn't! And I . . . I didn't!*

This is why Jesus warns:

> *"But if that wicked servant says to himself, 'My master is delayed,' and begins to beat his fellow servants*

and eats and drinks with drunkards, the master of that
servant will come on a day when he does not expect
him and at an hour he does not know and will cut
him in pieces and put him with the hypocrites. In that
place there will be weeping and gnashing of teeth."
—Matthew 24:48-51 ESV

The Church today, especially the church in the United States, the most powerful and influential nation on Earth, is at a final crossroads. Will the Church in America continue to increasingly embrace a "feel-good" gospel that encourages us in our success and enjoyment of this world, or will we lay down earthly treasures to seek and save the lost so that as few as possible are left after the Rapture?

OVERFLOW

Once Daniel realized it was time for the end of his exile, he didn't sit idly, waiting to be returned to the Promised Land. Instead, he turned to the throne of God in prayer and fasting and asked for forgiveness for his nation. He also prayed that once Israel was restored, the people might remember the fear of the Lord and not turn away from God again.

I believe this is why the first parable Jesus relates after challenging the disciples to be faithful and wise servants is of the ten virgins awaiting the coming of the bridegroom.

"Then the kingdom of heaven will be comparable to
ten virgins, who took their lamps and went out to meet
the bridegroom. Five of them were foolish, and five were
prudent. For when the foolish took their lamps, they
took no oil with them, but the prudent took oil in flasks
along with their lamps. Now while the bridegroom was

delaying, they all got drowsy and began to sleep. But at midnight there was a shout, 'Behold, the bridegroom! Come out to meet him.' Then all those virgins rose and trimmed their lamps. The foolish said to the prudent, 'Give us some of your oil, for our lamps are going out.' But the prudent answered, 'No, there will not be enough for us and you too; go instead to the dealers and buy some for yourselves.' And while they were going away to make the purchase, the bridegroom came, and those who were ready went in with him to the wedding feast; and the door was shut. Later the other virgins also came, saying, 'Lord, lord, open up for us.' But he answered, 'Truly I say to you, I do not know you.' Be on the alert then, for you do not know the day nor the hour."—Matthew 25:1-13

Throughout the Scriptures, oil is symbolic of the Holy Spirit. When we are born again, we are given a measure of the Holy Spirit that transforms our human spirit from spiritual death to spiritual life. (See John 20:22-23.) Then Paul writes that this is not enough. We must also *"be filled with the Spirit"* (Ephesians 5:18). The form of the verb *filled* here is in present continuous, which means "to be filled" like wind filling a sail, which makes the ship move. It is not one filling at one time but a continuous, moment-by-moment filling, all the time moving us forward in God's will for our lives.

The foolish virgins had just enough of the Holy Spirit to get through normal times. When they reached the limit of what was needed to get along in the world, they had no more. The wise virgins, however, had supplies in excess of what they needed. They had an overflow of the Spirit to face the trying times of waiting on God. Because of this, they entered into the marriage supper when the bridegroom arrived—the foolish virgins did not.

I believe that part of the reason we have seen a revival of praise and worship as well as a renewed dedication to 24-7 prayer in the last decade is because, as we enter the last of the latter days, we need to have twice as much of the presence of the Holy Spirit as we have needed up to this point.

Look at what the prophet Joel advised as he looked ahead to the last days:

> *Consecrate a fast, Proclaim a solemn assembly; Gather the elders And all the inhabitants of the land To the house of the Lord your God, And cry out to the Lord. Alas for the day! For the day of the Lord is near, And it will come as destruction from the Almighty.—Joel 1:14-15*

And then later:

> *"Yet even now," declares the LORD, "Return to Me with all your heart, And with fasting, weeping and mourning; And rend your heart and not your garments." Now return to the Lord your God, For He is gracious and compassionate, Slow to anger, abounding in lovingkindness And relenting of evil. Who knows whether He will not turn and relent And leave a blessing behind Him, Even a grain offering and a drink offering For the Lord your God? Blow a trumpet in Zion, Consecrate a fast, proclaim a solemn assembly, Gather the people, sanctify the congregation, Assemble the elders, Gather the children and the nursing infants. Let the bridegroom come out of his room And the bride out of her bridal chamber. Let the priests, the LORD's ministers, Weep between the porch and the altar, And let them say, "Spare Your people, O LORD, And do not make Your inheritance a reproach, A byword among the nations. Why should they among the peoples say, 'Where is their God?'"—Joel 2:12-17*

As Daniel fervently prayed when he saw his nation approach the end of a prophetic period, we need to pray fervently as we near the end of the Church Age. Adam failed in his God-given assignment to prolong Eden upon the Earth, and the Jews failed to live righteously before God as a nation dedicated to Him. Now let us, the Church, learn from their mistakes and not end our age of responsibility wondering if—or worse, regretting that—we could have done more.

SITTING ON OUR TALENTS?

Jesus follows The Parable of the Ten Virgins with the well-known Parable of the Talents. However, I want you to look at it again in this new light. When you heard it last used in a sermon, did the preacher mention that it was referring to how we occupy the Earth during the Church Age, before our Master returns? Look at the parable as Luke recorded it and see how Jesus brings out His points about the end of the age.

> *While they were listening to these things, Jesus went on to tell a parable, because He was near Jerusalem, and they supposed that the kingdom of God was going to appear immediately. So He said, "A nobleman went to a distant country to receive a kingdom for himself, and then return. And he called ten of his slaves, and gave them ten minas and said to them, 'Do business with this until I come back.'* [Occupy until I come. KJV] *But his citizens hated him and sent a delegation after him, saying, 'We do not want this man to reign over us.' When he returned, after receiving the kingdom, he ordered that these slaves, to whom he had given the money, be called to him so that he might know what business they had done. The first appeared, saying, 'Master, your mina has made ten minas more.' And he*

said to him, 'Well done, good slave, because you have been faithful in a very little thing, you are to be in authority over ten cities.' The second came, saying, 'Your mina, master, has made five minas.' And he said to him also, 'And you are to be over five cities.' Another came, saying, 'Master, here is your mina, which I kept put away in a handkerchief; for I was afraid of you, because you are an exacting man; you take up what you did not lay down and reap what you did not sow.' He said to him, 'By your own words I will judge you, you worthless slave. Did you know that I am an exacting man, taking up what I did not lay down and reaping what I did not sow? 'Then why did you not put my money in the bank, and having come, I would have collected it with interest?' Then he said to the bystanders, 'Take the mina away from him and give it to the one who has the ten minas.' And they said to him, 'Master, he has ten minas already.' I tell you that to everyone who has, more shall be given, but from the one who does not have, even what he does have shall be taken away. But these enemies of mine, who did not want me to reign over them, bring them here and slay them in my presence."—Luke 19:11-27

Each of us has been given things to invest—time, talents, treasures—and we are responsible to God for how we use them. We are to multiply our resources but also remember the moral of the Parable of the Unfaithful Steward in Luke 16:1-13: It is not as much about the money we make as it is about the friends we make along the way. *"I say to you, make friends for yourselves by means of the wealth of unrighteousness, so that when it fails, they will receive you into the eternal dwellings"* (Luke 16:9).

In the parable, Jesus says that when He returns to set up His kingdom, those who are faithful in this way will be given authority over *cities* in the kingdom. This seems to be a blessing for the millennial reign. Those who do the best job in spreading the kingdom of God and manage caring for "*the least of these*" (Matthew 25:45) will be the ones tapped to oversee the millennial kingdom created after Jesus returns.

UNTO THE LEAST OF THESE

In closing, Jesus describes the final judgment day. The criterion for blessing or cursing on that day will not be the size of our churches or how many television stations carry our services but the lowest common denominators of life: What did we do about those in greatest need?

> *"But when the Son of Man comes in His glory, and all the angels with Him, then He will sit on His glorious throne. All the nations will be gathered before Him; and He will separate them from one another, as the shepherd separates the sheep from the goats; and He will put the sheep on His right, and the goats on the left.*
>
> *"Then the King will say to those on His right, 'Come, you who are blessed of My Father, inherit the kingdom prepared for you from the foundation of the world. 'For I was hungry, and you gave Me something to eat; I was thirsty, and you gave Me something to drink; I was a stranger, and you invited Me in; naked, and you clothed Me; I was sick, and you visited Me; I was in prison, and you came to Me.' Then the righteous will answer Him, 'Lord, when did we see You hungry, and feed You, or thirsty, and give You something to drink? 'And when did we see You a stranger, and invite You in, or naked, and clothe You? 'When did we see You sick, or in prison, and come to You?' The King will answer and say to them, 'Truly I say to you, to the*

*extent that you did it to one of these brothers of Mine,
even the least of them, you did it to Me.'*

*"Then He will also say to those on His left, 'Depart
from Me, accursed ones, into the eternal fire which has
been prepared for the devil and his angels; for I was
hungry, and you gave Me nothing to eat; I was thirsty,
and you gave Me nothing to drink; I was a stranger, and
you did not invite Me in; naked, and you did not clothe
Me; sick, and in prison, and you did not visit Me.' Then
they themselves also will answer, 'Lord, when did we see
You hungry, or thirsty, or a stranger, or naked, or sick,
or in prison, and did not take care of You?' Then He will
answer them, 'Truly I say to you, to the extent that you
did not do it to one of the least of these, you did not do
it to Me.' These will go away into eternal punishment,
but the righteous into eternal life."—Matthew 25:31-46*

The evils being perpetrated on humanity in the twenty-first
century are not difficult to discern, and in many cases the means of
alleviating them are already in place. Millions lack clean water, the
simplest means of disease prevention that would save untold numbers
of children. The number of widows and orphans in need is at an all-
time high due to wars, AIDS, and persecution. There are more slaves in
the world today than were ever taken out of Africa to America and the
British Realm before the U.S. Civil War. More than half of these slaves
today are children, many who are being sexually exploited. Famine,
pestilence, and ignorance still rule many nations, allowing them to be
manipulated by unscrupulous terrorists who sacrifice young lives for
their own evil agendas.

At the same time, the fields are white for harvest and in need of
laborers. We are the generation of the final stand! Will we be content

to hide within the walls of our churches and simply survive the coming events, or will we take the fight to the gates of Hell as Jesus said we could in Matthew 16:18?

BEING PART OF THE FINAL GENERATION

Know this first of all, that in the last days mockers will come with their mocking, following after their own lusts, and saying, "Where is the promise of His coming? For ever since the fathers fell asleep, all continues just as it was from the beginning of creation."—2 Peter 3:3-4

Just before his dying breath, Peter exhorted us in the verses above that the first and foremost thing to remember in the last days was this: Don't fall for the lie that Jesus is not coming soon! And by now, I hope you can feel the urgency with which I write. Certainly wiser teachers than I have looked at these scriptures and the signs of their generation, declared that Jesus was coming within days or a couple of years at most—and to this point have all been proven wrong. Perhaps I will be as well. However, it is impossible to look at all of these things together as they are happening today and not feel we are in a pivotal time, a time such as Daniel faced as he read the Scriptures and recognized the imminent end of a prophetic age.

Change is in the air in so many ways today, and whether that will be change for the better or for the worse is in the hands of this generation. We cannot wait for another. The future of freedom in the Middle East and who wins between the Shia Twelvers of Iran and the democracies of the United States and Israel will not be put off for another decade. As Egypt, Tunisia, Yemen, Libya, and even Syria, Jordan, and Bahrain look for a freer, more self-determined future for their nations, it is uncertain whether they will find what the former Eastern Bloc countries found when the USSR crumbled or be swallowed by radical Islam as Iran was after the Shah fell. We must stand for what is right, pray for the peace of Jerusalem, bless and be a blessing to Israel, and then put into action the things God places in our hearts to do.

There is much to accomplish before the Master returns! Will He find us faithful and wise when He comes, or will He catch us unaware, living the life of indulgent consumers? Will we continue on the selfish, self-centered path that is lulling America to sleep as liberalism and debt swallow the liberties for which our forefathers fought? I hope and pray not! I believe the prophets of God are sounding the alarm and His people are awakening. If just a remnant, we are arising to shake off our flesh, fill our lamps with an abundance of oil, and march forward to do God's will for our lives—which will ultimately bring in the greatest harvest the world has ever seen—and bring our glorious Lord and Savior back to Earth.

Godspeed in your end-times mission!

He who testifies to these things

says, "Yes, I am coming quickly."

Amen. Come, Lord Jesus.

The grace of the Lord Jesus

be with all. Amen.

—REVELATION 22:20-21

A TIMETABLE OF PROPHETIC EVENTS

605 BC	Northern Kingdom of Israel conquered by the Assyrians (then immediately conquered by Nebuchadnezzar); Daniel, Hananiah (Shadrach), Mishael (Meshach), Azariah (Abednego), and other Jewish youths are taken as captives to Babylon (Daniel was likely in his twenties)
604 BC	Daniel receives a vision of Nebuchadnezzar's dream, which is the statue of gold, silver, bronze, iron, and iron/clay, representing the five world-empires that will rule the Middle East: Babylon, Medo-Persia, Greece, Rome, and the one that will rise up out of the land of ancient Rome to rule in the Tribulation
586 BC	Nebuchadnezzar conquers Jerusalem and destroys it and the Temple The Southern Kingdom of Judah is carried into captivity Judah's 70 years of exile begin
586 BC	Ezekiel records chapters 36-39, foretelling the rebirth of the nation of Israel and the subsequent battle of Gog and Magog
circa 550 BC	Persia is born under Cyrus the Great
539 BC	Persia conquers Babylon
538 BC	Daniel survives the lion's den First year of Darius I as governor over the Babylonian territory Daniel prays (Daniel 9) and receives the vision of the 70 weeks
circa 520 BC	Foundation of the Second Temple is completed End of Israel's 70 years of exile
circa 445 BC	Artaxerxes decrees Jerusalem can be rebuilt (Nehemiah 2:8) Beginning of the 70 Weeks of Daniel (Daniel 9:24-27)
396 BC	Rebuilding of Jerusalem and the Temple is completed (no historical verification available) End of the 1st Week of Daniel
175-164 BC	Rule of Antiochus IV Epiphanes, the first "dress rehearsal" of an Antichrist—"the prince who is to come" (foretold in Daniel 11:21-35)
circa AD 0	Jesus' First Coming

circa AD 32	Jesus' death on the Cross and resurrection The end of the first 69 of Daniel's 70 Weeks Jesus' ascension to the right hand of the Father and the gift of the Holy Spirit to the Church; prophetic countdown pauses at 69 Weeks Church Age Begins
AD 70	Destruction of the Temple and Jerusalem
AD 135	Rebellion of Bar Kokhba Diaspora (scattering of the Jews to the nations of the Earth)
AD 622	Birth of Islam
AD 632	Death of Muhammad
AD 638	Muslim conquest of Palestine
1099-1187	Reign of Christian Crusaders in Middle East
1187	Saladin violates his cease-fire agreement with the Crusaders and launches a surprise attack that allows him to capture Jerusalem
1730	First synagogue in New York
1798	Napoleon arrives in Egypt—beginning of modern Western subjugation of the Muslim world
1840	The Damascus Incident
1844	George Bush publishes The Valley of Vision
1881-1924	2.5 million Jews flee persecution in Eastern Europe
1882	Sir Robert Anderson's first edition of The Coming Prince published
1887	Blackstone's Jesus Is Coming published
1891	Blackstone presents his Memorial to President Harrison
1897	First Zionist Congress
Nov. 2, 1917	The Balfour Declaration, in which the United Kingdom commits to the establishment of a Jewish homeland in Palestine
1918	End of World War I; disintegration of the Ottoman Empire; the area becomes known as the British Mandate for Palestine
1928	Founding of Muslim Brotherhood
1929	Arab mobs slaughter Jewish community in Hebron; British force survivors to evacuate

1933-45	Jewish Holocaust in Germany; Arab states and leaders join with Nazi Germany
1939	Britain issues White Paper reneging on its promise, as expressed in the Balfour Declaration, for a Jewish state in Palestine; this change in policy kept millions of European Jews from escaping Nazi-occupied Europe to Palestine
Nov. 29, 1947	Resolution 181 passed—the Partition of Palestine into Jewish and Arab states A civil war breaks out between Muslims and Jews in Palestine
May 14, 1948	Reunification of the Nation of Israel
1948	A quarter century after U.S. Congress' 1922 resolution calling for the establishment of a Jewish homeland, members of Congress speak out to buttress President Truman's decision to recognize the Jewish State, which begins U.S. congressional support for Israel
1949	A series of Armistice agreements are signed between Israel and Arab states to end the Israeli War of Independence
1951	U. S. Congress approves the first aid package to Israel; $65 million to help take in Holocaust survivors and endangered Jews from Arab Lands; within three years Israel's 650,000 Jews absorb 600,000 refugees from Europe and the Arab nations
1955	One-Third of the House of Representatives petitions the Eisenhower administration to break its arms embargo of Israel and sell defensive weapons to the Jewish state; although continued Congressional urging, U.S. embargo of Israel does not end until 1962 United States sells hundreds of millions of dollars in weapons to Arab states during the years of the Israel embargo
Oct. 1956	Suez War Crisis
1964	Establishment of the Palestine Liberation Organization (PLO)
June 5-11, 1967	Six-Day War
1970	70 senators and 289 representatives reject Secretary of State Rogers' peace plan, which calls for Israel's unilateral withdrawal without Arab peace commitments
Sept. 1972	Arafat's Black September organization murders 11 Israeli athletes at Olympic Games in Munich
Oct. 1973	Yom Kippur War
1973	71 senators and 269 representatives expedite air package to Israel, which President Nixon approves and is the first time the U.S. provides an outright grant of arms to Israel
1974	Yasser Arafat addresses the United Nations; U.N. General Assembly and Arab League recognize PLO as sole legitimate representative of the Palestinian people

1977	Egyptian President Anwar Sadat makes breakthrough visit to Israel
1979	Egypt and Israel sign peace treaty at Camp David with President Jimmy Carter looking on
1979	Soviets invade Afghanistan
1979	Ayatollah Khomeini returns to Iran
1979	Invasion of U.S. embassy in Tehran by Islamic militants and beginning of hostage situation
1980-88	Iran-Iraq War
1982	In the wake of the war in Lebanon, Reagan administration suspends the sale of F-16 planes to Israel and tries to cut aid; senate responds by increasing military aid and grants by $225 million, sending a strong message of its support of Israel
1981	Despite strong congressional opposition, AWACs planes are sold to Saudi Arabia
1982-85	War in Lebanon
1983	Strategic Cooperation Endorsement After 35 years of being excluded as a strategic partner (for fear of provoking Arab wrath), U.S. recognizes Israel as strategic asset in landmark Memorandum of Understanding; in future years Congress expands this relationship to recognize Israel as a major non-NATO ally to funding an array of U.S.-Israel joint research and defense programs in the anti-ballistic missile arena
1983	Formation of Hezbollah
1984	After a decade and a half of unmitigated PLO horror, U.S. Congress passes legislation that precludes dialogue with the PLO unless and until the PLO renounces terrorism; in future initiatives Congress acts to close the PLO office, denies Arafat an American visa, provides the U.S. with the legal authority to prosecute terrorists, and restricts U.S. dealings with nations supporting terror
1987	First Intifada (Palestinians against Israel)
1989	USSR withdraws from Afghanistan
1989	95 senators resist intense pressure for unilateral Israeli concessions and urge Secretary of State Baker to support Israel's peace efforts
Aug. 2, 1990	Iraq invades Kuwait
1991	The Gulf War: Madrid Peace Conference

1991	Israel endures 39 Iraqi missile attacks during the Gulf War without re-taliating; U.S. Congress approves $650 million in emergency assistance to Israel
Sept. 13, 1993	Oslo Peace Accords
1994	PLO establishes Palestinian Authority with Yasser Arafat as its head
1994	Israeli-Jordanian Peace Agreement
Sept. 28, 1995	Rabin and Arafat sign final Oslo II Agreement in Washington, D.C., with President Bill Clinton looking on
Nov. 5, 1995	Rabin assassinated
Nov. 22, 1995	Peres becomes prime minister of Israel
1996	Congress agrees to provide $100 million in anti-terror assistance to Israel; members of Congress also sign letters urging the Palestine Authority to take more serious steps against terror
Oct. 23, 1998	Netanyahu, Arafat, and Clinton sign the Wye River Memorandum at the Wye Accords
May 17, 1999	Ehud Barak wins the election in Israel
Nov. 1999	U.S.-Israeli-Palestinian trilateral summit in Oslo
Jan. 2000	Syrian-Israeli talks begin in Shepherdstown, WV; Clinton drafts "Shepherdstown Document"
Jan. 2000	Barak reopens negotiations with the Palestinian Authority that had stalled in early December; Israel agrees to withdraw from 5.1 percent of the West Bank and to release 22 Palestinian prisoners; Arafat changes demands for January 20 final withdrawal
Jan. 2000	U.S.-Israeli-Palestinian Authority trilateral summit at Camp David; summit fails after two weeks of intense negotiations when Arafat rejects unprecedented offer from Israel, in which Israel offered 94 percent of the occupied territories, part of East Jerusalem, and the return of tens of thousands of Palestinian family members; at this time, 98 percent of Palestinians in disputed territories live under Palestinian rule
2000	265 members of the House and 96 senators urge the Clinton administration to stand by Israel and press Arafat to end the violence Decades of cooperation between the U.S. and Israel to jointly develop missile defense results in Israeli development of the Arrow Missile defense system; Israel is the only country in the world to have a functioning defense against enemy missiles
Sept. 28, 2000	Perez visits Temple Mount; Second Intifada
Oct. 12, 2000	Islamist terrorists ram the USS Cole in Yemen

Sept. 11, 2001	Hijacked planes strike World Trade Center towers in New York; hijacked plane crashes into Pentagon in Washington D.C.; another hijacked plane crashes in Pennsylvania
Oct. 7, 2001	U.S. begins bombing Al-Qaeda and Taliban positions in Afghanistan
2002	Israeli army invades Jenin Refugee Camp, home to 14,000 Palestinian civilians, rendering 4,000 civilians homeless; Israel begins construction of its separation wall to enclose West Bank
2003	U.S.-led Roadmap to Peace is introduced
?	Gog's coalition of nations attack Israel but are thwarted by a super-natural intervention of God (The Battle of Gog and Magog)
?	As persecution arises, the greatest revival in history will sweep the Earth
?	The Rapture or Catching Away of the Church of Jesus Christ
?	The Antichrist's seven-year-peace pact with Israel Beginning of Daniel's 70th Week and the Tribulation
?	Rebuilding of the Temple
3.5 years into the Tribulation	The Temple's desecration by the Antichrist (The Abomination of Desecration) Midpoint of the Tribulation and the beginning of the Great Tribulation
7 Years into the Tribulation	The Battle of Armageddon The end of Daniel's 70th Week End of the world averted by Jesus' Second Coming
?	The Millennium
?	The Great White Throne of Judgment
?	New Heaven and new Earth created; New Jerusalem descends from God
?	Eternity

THE SIGNS OF MATTHEW 24 ACROSS THREE GOSPELS

Matthew 24	Mark 13	Luke 17	Luke 21
[1] Jesus came out from the temple and was going away when His disciples came up to point out the temple buildings to Him. [2] And He said to them, "Do you not see all these things? Truly I say to you, not one stone here will be left upon another, which will not be torn down."	[1] As He was going out of the temple, one of His disciples said to Him, "Teacher, behold what wonderful stones and what wonderful buildings!" [2] And Jesus said to him, "Do you see these great buildings? Not one stone will be left upon another which will not be torn down."		
[3] As He was sitting on the Mount of Olives, the disciples came to Him privately, saying, "Tell us, when will these things happen, and what will be the sign of Your coming, and of the end of the age?"	[3] As He was sitting on the Mount of Olives opposite the temple, Peter and James and John and Andrew were questioning Him privately, [4] "Tell us, when will these things be, and what will be the sign when all these things are going to be fulfilled?"		
[4] And Jesus answered and said to them, "See to it that no one misleads you. [5] For many will come in My name, saying, 'I am the Christ,' and will mislead many.	[5] And Jesus began to say to them, "See to it that no one misleads you. [6] Many will come in My name, saying, 'I am He!' and will mislead many.		
[6] "You will be hearing of wars and rumors of wars. See that you are not frightened, for those things must take place, but that is not yet the end. [7] For nation will rise against nation, and kingdom against kingdom,	[7] "When you hear of wars and rumors of wars, do not be frightened; those things must take place; but that is not yet the end. [8] For nation will rise up against nation, and kingdom against kingdom;		[10] Then He continued by saying to them, "Nation will rise against nation and kingdom against kingdom,

Matthew 24	Mark 13	Luke 17	Luke 21
and in various places there will be famines and earthquakes. [8] But all these things are merely the beginning of birth pangs.	there will be earthquakes in various places; there will also be famines. These things are merely the beginning of birth pangs.		[11] and there will be great earthquakes, and in various places plagues and famines; and there will be terrors and great signs from heaven.
[9] "Then they will deliver you to tribulation, and will kill you, and you will be hated by all nations because of My name.	[9] "But be on your guard; for they will deliver you to the courts, and you will be flogged in the synagogues, and you will stand before governors and kings for My sake, as a testimony to them. [10] The gospel must first be preached to all the nations. [11] When they arrest you and hand you over, do not worry beforehand about what you are to say, but say whatever is given you in that hour; for it is not you who speak, but it is the Holy Spirit. [12] Brother will betray brother to death, and a father his child; and children will rise up against parents and have them put to death.		[12] "But before all these things, they will lay their hands on you and will persecute you, delivering you to the synagogues and prisons, bringing you before kings and governors for My name's sake. [13] It will lead to an opportunity for your testimony. [14] So make up your minds not to prepare beforehand to defend yourselves; [15] for I will give you utterance and wisdom which none of your opponents will be able to resist or refute. [16] But you will be betrayed even by parents and brothers and relatives and friends, and they will put some of you to death, [17] and you will be hated by all because of My name.
[10] "At that time many will fall away and will betray one another and hate one another. [11] Many false prophets will arise and will mislead many. [12] Because lawlessness is increased, most people's love will grow cold.			
[13] "But the one who endures to the end, he will be saved.	[13] "You will be hated by all because of My name, but the one who endures to the end, he will be saved.		[18] "Yet not a hair of your head will perish. [19] By your endurance you will gain your lives.

Matthew 24	Mark 13	Luke 17	Luke 21
[14] "This gospel of the kingdom shall be preached in the whole world as a testimony to all the nations, and then the end will come.			
[15] "Therefore when you see the ABOMINATION OF DESOLATION which was spoken of through Daniel the prophet, standing in the holy place (let the reader understand), [16] then those who are in Judea must flee to the mountains. [17] Whoever is on the housetop must not go down to get the things out that are in his house. [18] Whoever is in the field must not turn back to get his cloak. [19] But woe to those who are pregnant and to those who are nursing babies in those days! [20] But pray that your flight will not be in the winter, or on a Sabbath.	[14] "But when you see the ABOMINATION OF DESOLATION standing where it should not be (let the reader understand), then those who are in Judea must flee to the mountains. [15] The one who is on the housetop must not go down, or go in to get anything out of his house; [16] and the one who is in the field must not turn back to get his coat. [17] But woe to those who are pregnant and to those who are nursing babies in those days! [18] But pray that it may not happen in the winter.		[20] "But when you see Jerusalem surrounded by armies, then recognize that her desolation is near. [21] Then those who are in Judea must flee to the mountains, and those who are in the midst of the city must leave, and those who are in the country must not enter the city; [22] because these are days of vengeance, so that all things which are written will be fulfilled. [23] Woe to those who are pregnant and to those who are nursing babies in those days; for there will be great distress upon the land and wrath to this people; [24] and they will fall by the edge of the sword, and will be led captive into all the nations; and Jerusalem will be trampled underfoot by the Gentiles until the times of the Gentiles are fulfilled.
[21] "For then there will be a great tribulation, such as has not occurred since the beginning of the world until now, nor ever will.	[19] "For those days will be a time of tribulation such as has not occurred since the beginning of the creation which God created until now, and never will.		

Matthew 24	Mark 13	Luke 17	Luke 21
[22] "Unless those days had been cut short, no life would have been saved; but for the sake of the elect those days will be cut short.	[20] "Unless the Lord had shortened those days, no life would have been saved; but for the sake of the elect, whom He chose, He shortened the days.		
[23] "Then if anyone says to you, 'Behold, here is the Christ,' or 'There He is,' do not believe him. [24] For false Christs and false prophets will arise and will show great signs and wonders, so as to mislead, if possible, even the elect.	[21] "And then if anyone says to you, 'Behold, here is the Christ'; or, 'Behold, He is there'; do not believe him; [22] for false Christs and false prophets will arise, and will show signs and wonders, in order to lead astray, if possible, the elect.		
[25] "Behold, I have told you in advance.	[23] "But take heed; behold, I have told you everything in advance.		
[26] "So if they say to you, 'Behold, He is in the wilderness,' do not go out, or, 'Behold, He is in the inner rooms,' do not believe them.		[22] And He said to the disciples, "The days will come when you will long to see one of the days of the Son of Man, and you will not see it. [23] They will say to you, 'Look there! Look here!' Do not go away, and do not run after them.	
[27] "For just as the lightning comes from the east and flashes even to the west, so will the coming of the Son of Man be.		[24] "For just like the lightning, when it flashes out of one part of the sky, shines to the other part of the sky, so will the Son of Man be in His day.	
		[25] "But first He must suffer many things and be rejected by this generation.	
[28] "Wherever the corpse is, there the vultures will gather.			

Matthew 24	Mark 13	Luke 17	Luke 21
29 "But immediately after the tribulation of those days THE SUN WILL BE DARKENED, AND THE MOON WILL NOT GIVE ITS LIGHT, AND THE STARS WILL FALL from the sky, and the powers of the heavens will be shaken.	24 "But in those days, after that tribulation, THE SUN WILL BE DARK-ENED AND THE MOON WILL NOT GIVE ITS LIGHT, 25 AND THE STARS WILL BE FALLING from heaven, and the powers that are in the heavens will be shaken.		25 "There will be signs in sun and moon and stars, and on the earth dismay among nations, in per-plexity at the roaring of the sea and the waves, 26 men fainting from fear and the expectation of the things which are coming upon the world; for the powers of the heavens will be shaken.
30 "And then the sign of the Son of Man will ap-pear in the sky, and then all the tribes of the earth will mourn, and they will see the SON OF MAN COMING ON THE CLOUDS OF THE SKY with power and great glory.	26 "Then they will see THE SON OF MAN COMING IN CLOUDS with great power and glory.		27 "Then they will see THE SON OF MAN COMING IN A CLOUD with power and great glory.
31 "And He will send forth His angels with A GREAT TRUMPET and THEY WILL GATHER TOGETHER His elect from the four winds, from one end of the sky to the other.	27 "And then He will send forth the angels, and will gather together His elect from the four winds, from the farthest end of the earth to the farthest end of heaven.		28 "But when these things begin to take place, straighten up and lift up your heads, because your redemption is draw-ing near."
32 "Now learn the parable from the fig tree: when its branch has already become tender and puts forth its leaves, you know that summer is near; 33 so, you too, when you see all these things, recognize that He is near, right at the door.	28 "Now learn the parable from the fig tree: when its branch has already become tender and puts forth its leaves, you know that summer is near. 29 Even so, you too, when you see these things happening, recog-nize that He is near, right at the door.		29 Then He told them a parable: "Behold the fig tree and all the trees; 30 as soon as they put forth leaves, you see it and know for yourselves that summer is now near. 31 So you also, when you see these things happen-ing, recognize that the kingdom of God is near.
34 "Truly I say to you, this generation will not pass away until all these things take place.	30 "Truly I say to you, this generation will not pass away until all these things take place.		32 "Truly I say to you, this generation will not pass away until all things take place.
35 "Heaven and earth will pass away, but My words will not pass away.	31 "Heaven and earth will pass away, but My words will not pass away.		33 "Heaven and earth will pass away, but My words will not pass away.

Matthew 24	Mark 13	Luke 17	Luke 21
[36] "But of that day and hour no one knows, not even the angels of heaven, nor the Son, but the Father alone.	[32] "But of that day or hour no one knows, not even the angels in heaven, nor the Son, but the Father alone.		
[37] "For the coming of the Son of Man will be just like the days of Noah. [38] For as in those days before the flood they were eating and drinking, marrying and giving in marriage, until the day that Noah entered the ark, [39] and they did not understand until the flood came and took them all away; so will the coming of the Son of Man be.		[26] "And just as it happened in the days of Noah, so it will be also in the days of the Son of Man: [27] they were eating, they were drinking, they were marrying, they were being given in marriage, until the day that Noah entered the ark, and the flood came and destroyed them all.	
		[28] "It was the same as happened in the days of Lot: they were eating, they were drinking, they were buying, they were selling, they were planting, they were building; [29] but on the day that Lot went out from Sodom it rained fire and brimstone from heaven and destroyed them all. [30] It will be just the same on the day that the Son of Man is revealed.	
		[31] "On that day, the one who is on the housetop and whose goods are in the house must not go down to take them out; and likewise the one who is in the field must not turn back.	
		[32] "Remember Lot's wife. [33] Whoever seeks to keep his life will lose it, and whoever loses his life will preserve it.	

Matthew 24	Mark 13	Luke 17	Luke 21
[40] "Then there will be two men in the field; one will be taken and one will be left. [41] Two women will be grinding at the mill; one will be taken and one will be left.		[34] "I tell you, on that night there will be two in one bed; one will be taken and the other will be left. [35] "There will be two women grinding at the same place; one will be taken and the other will be left. [36] ["Two men will be in the field; one will be taken and the other will be left."]	
		[37] And answering they said to Him, "Where, Lord?" And He said to them, "Where the body is, there also the vultures will be gathered."	
[42] "Therefore be on the alert, for you do not know which day your Lord is coming.	[33] "Take heed, keep on the alert; for you do not know when the appointed time will come.		[34] "Be on guard, so that your hearts will not be weighted down with dissipation and drunkenness and the worries of life, and that day will not come on you suddenly like a trap; [35] for it will come upon all those who dwell on the face of all the earth.
[43] "But be sure of this, that if the head of the house had known at what time of the night the thief was coming, he would have been on the alert and would not have allowed his house to be broken into. [44] For this reason you also must be ready; for the Son of Man is coming at an hour when you do not think He will.			

Matthew 24	Mark 13	Luke 17	Luke 21
[45] "Who then is the faithful and sensible slave whom his master put in charge of his household to give them their food at the proper time? [46] Blessed is that slave whom his master finds so doing when he comes. [47] Truly I say to you that he will put him in charge of all his possessions. [48] But if that evil slave says in his heart, 'My master is not coming for a long time,' [49] and begins to beat his fellow slaves and eat and drink with drunkards; [50] the master of that slave will come on a day when he does not expect him and at an hour which he does not know, [51] and will cut him in pieces and assign him a place with the hypocrites; in that place there will be weeping and gnashing of teeth."	[34] "It is like a man away on a journey, who upon leaving his house and putting his slaves in charge, assigning to each one his task, also commanded the doorkeeper to stay on the alert.		
	[35] "Therefore, be on the alert—for you do not know when the master of the house is coming, whether in the evening, at midnight, or when the rooster crows, or in the morning— [36] in case he should come suddenly and find you asleep. [37] What I say to you I say to all, 'Be on the alert!'"		[36] "But keep on the alert at all times, praying that you may have strength to escape all these things that are about to take place, and to stand before the Son of Man."

BIBLIOGRAPHY

_____. *The Coming Is Upon Us*. "Iran Leaders: The Coming is Upon Us – Israel Shall be Destroyed! (Watch the Video)." A Time to Betray website. Streaming video, (March 28, 2011). http://atimetobetray.com/blog/iran-leaders-the-coming-is-upon-us---israel-shall-be-destroyed-watch-the-video/.

_____. "Human Rights First Condemns Passage of U.N. Resolution 'Combating Defamation of Religions.'" Human Rights *First* press release (December 21, 2010). http://www.humanrightsfirst.org/2010/12/21/human-rights-first-condemns-passage-of-u-n-resolution-"combating-defamation-of-religions"/.

_____. "Islamic Mobs Burn Down Church in Egypt," *Compass Direct* (March 8, 2011), http://www.compassdirect.org/english/country/egypt/69546/.

_____. "Investment Banking Jobs—Vice Presidents or Directors." *Trades and Tombstones* website (2009). http://investmentbanking.jobsearchdigest.com/97/investment-banking-jobs-vice-president-or-director/.

_____. "Murder of Governor in Pakistan Darkens 'Blasphemy' Case." *Compass Direct News* (January 5, 2011). http://www.compassdirect.org/english/country/pakistan/30961/.

_____. "Obama promises king Israel will withdraw from West Bank, Jerusalem." Geostrategy-Direct.com (July 7, 2010). http://www.geostrategy-direct.com/geostrategy-direct/. (Accessed July 2010).

_____. "Right to Believe." Open Doors UK website. http://www.opendoorsuk.org/campaign/RTB.php (Accessed: February 18, 2011).

_____. "Report: Egypt has approved Iran warships to use Suez Canal." *Haaretz.com* (February 18, 2011). http://www.haaretz.com/news/international/report-egypt-has-approved-iran-warships-to-use-suez-canal-1.344310.

_____. "Six Megathemes Emerge from Barna Group Research in 2010." Barna Group Research (December 13, 2010). http://www.barna.org/culture-articles/462-six-megathemes-emerge-from-2010.

_____. "Social Security Benefit Amounts." Social Security online (last updated: October 29, 2010). http://www.ssa.gov/oact/cola/Benefits.html.

_____. *This American Life*, "423: The Invention of Money." *National Public Radio* (January 7, 2011). Audio, available at: http://www.thisamericanlife.org/radio-archives/episode/423/the-invention-of-money.

_____. *The Treasury of Scripture Knowledge: Five Hundred Thousand Scripture References and Parallel Passages.*. Oak Harbor, WA: Logos Research Systems, Inc., 1995.

_____. "US, Israel Will Soon Exit the Middle East: Ahmadinejad." *France 24* (February 11, 2011). http://www.france24.com/en/20110211-us-israel-will-soon-exit-middle-east-ahmadinejad.

_____. "Yom Kippur War: Sacrificial Stand in the Golan Heights." *HistoryNet.com* (June 12, 2006). http://www.historynet.com/yom-kippur-war-sacrificial-stand-in-the-golan-heights.htm/1.

_____. "Combating Defamation of Religion." Available at http://www.eyeontheun.org/developments-item.asp?d=9299&rid=12464 (Accessed: February 18, 2011).

Ahmadinejad, Mahmoud. "Address by H.E. Dr. Mahmoud Ahmadinejad, President of the Islamic Republic of Iran Before the 65th Session of the United Nations General Assembly." September 23, 2010. http://www.un.org/en/ga/65/meetings/generaldebate/Portals/1/statements/634208557381562500IR_en.pdf.

Associated Press. "New Round of Mideast Peace Talks Begin." *Las Vegas Sun* (September 9, 2010). http://www.google.com/search?sourceid=navclient&ie=UTF-8&rlz=1T4GGLL_enUS382US382&q=I+see+in+you+a+partner+for+peace.

Associated Press. "Poll: Over Half of Egypt Wants End to Israel Peace." *NewsMax.com* (April 25, 2011). http://www.newsmax.com/Newsfront/ML-Egypt-Poll/2011/04/25/id/394043.

Anderson, Robert. *The Coming Prince: The Marvelous Prophecy of Daniel's Seventy Weeks Concerning the Antichrist*. Amazon Digital Services, 1882.

Anderson, Troy. "A Jewish Awakening?" *Charisma* magazine website (December 9, 2010). http://www.charismamag.com/index.php/newsletters/standing-with-israel/29723-a-jewish-awakening-.

Ayalon, Danny. Interview with Joel Rosenberg during "Assessing the Threat of Radical Islam in the Epicenter." Streaming video, Epicenter Conference 2011 (May 16, 2011). http://www.epicenterconference.com/.

Barrett, David B. and Johnson, Todd M. "Annual Statistical Table on Global Mission: 2004," *International Bulletin of Missionary Research*, Vol. 28, No. 1 (January 2004).

Barrett, David B. and Johnson, Todd M. "Christianity 2011: Martyrs and the Resurgence of Religion," *International Bulletin of Missionary Research* (January 2011).

Barrett, David B. and Johnson, Todd M. *World Christian Trends AD 30–AD 2200: Interpreting the Annual Christian Megacensus*. Pasadena, CA: William Carey Library, 2001.

Bentley, Ray. "Drawing Lessons from the Book of Joel for Israel, the Church, and the Nations," Epicenter Conference 2011 (May 15, 2011). A panel discussion moderated by Joel Rosenberg, streaming video, http://www.epicenterconference.com/.

Bentley, Ray. "Joel 2:1-17: A Trumpet Call for Israel and the Church." *Epicenter Conference 2011* (May 15, 2011). Streaming video, http://www.epicenterconference.com/.

Blackstone, William E. *Jesus Is Coming: God's Hope for a Restless World*. Grand Rapids, MI: Kregel Classics, 1989.

Borenstien, Seth and Reed Bell, Julie. "2010 Extreme Weather: Deadliest Year in a Generation," *The Huffington Post* (December 22, 2010). http://www.huffingtonpost.com/2010/12/20/2010-extreme-weather-dead_n_798956.html.

Brahic, Catherine. "The megaquake connection: Are huge earthquakes linked?" *New Scientist* (March 16, 2011). http://www.newscientist.com/article/mg20928043.000-the-megaquake-connection-are-huge-earthquakes-linked.html.

Bronner, Ethan. "Gas Field Confirmed Off Coast of Israel." *New York Times* (December 30, 2010). http://www.nytimes.com/2010/12/31/world/middleeast/31leviathan.html?_r=2.

Burrough, Bryan; Loeb, Allan; and Schiff, Stephen. *Wall Street II: Money Never Sleeps*. DVD, directed by Oliver Stone. Twentieth Century Fox, 2010.

Bush, George. *The Valley of Vision; or The Dry Bones of Israel Revived: An Attempted Proof (From Ezekiel, Chapter 37:1-14) of the Restoration and Conversion of the Jews*. New York: Saxton & Miles, 1844.

Cooper, Helene. "Obama and Netanyahu, Distrustful Allies, Meet." *New York Times* (May 19, 2011). http://www.nytimes.com/2011/05/20/world/middleeast/20policy.html?_r=2&WT.mc_id=NYT-E-I-NYT-E-AT-0525-L17&pagewanted=all.

Doyle, Tom. *Breakthrough: The Return of Hope to the Middle East*. Colorado Springs, CO: Authentic Publishing, 2008.

Evans-Pritchard, Ambrose. "The Death of Paper Money." *The Telegraph* (July 25, 2010). http://www.telegraph.co.uk/finance/comment/ambroseevans_pritchard/7909432/The-Death-of-Paper-Money.html.

Fergusson, Adam. *When Money Dies: The Nightmare of Deficit Spending, Devaluation, and Hyperinflation in Weimar Germany*. New York: PublicAffairs, 1975.

Ferguson, Charles. *Inside Job*. DVD, directed by Charles Ferguson. Sony Picture Classics, 2010.

Gaines, Adrienne S. "Company Claims 1.5 Billion Barrels of Oil Found in Israel." *Charisma News Online* (August 19, 2010). http://www.charismamag.com/index.php/news/29124-company-claims-15-billion-barrels-of-oil-found-in-israel.

Goodrich, Frances et al. *It's A Wonderful Life*. DVD, directed by Frank Capra. New York: RKO Pictures, 1946.

Guerin, Orla. "Fear for Pakistan's Death Row Christian Woman," *BBC News* (December 5, 2010). http://www.bbc.co.uk/news/world-south-asia-11923701.

Guynn, Jessica. "Google exec Wael Ghonim in Egypt says long live the revolution 2.0." Los Angeles Times website (February 11, 2011). http://latimesblogs.latimes.com/technology/2011/02/google-exec-wael-ghonim-in-egypt-says-long-live-the-revolution-20.html.

Hybels, Bill and Bono. "Bill Hybels and Bono 1." YouTube (April 10, 2008). http://www.youtube.com/watch?v=grBByc7t3Fs.

Jennings, Audra. "The Breakthrough of Christianity in the Middle East: Q & A with Tom Doyle, Author of *Breakthrough*." Christian Post Blogs (March 27, 2009). http://blogs.christianpost.com/books/2009/03/the-breakthrough-of-christianity-in-the-middle-east-27/.

Johnson, Simon. "The Quiet Coup." *The Atlantic Monthly* (May 2009). http://www.theatlantic.com/magazine/print/2009/05/the-quiet-coup/7364/.

Kahlil, Reza. Interview with Joel Rosenberg presented during "Assessing the Threat of Radical Islam in the Epicenter." Epicenter Conference 2011, streaming video, (May 16, 2011). http://www.epicenterconference.com/.

Kempinski, Lev & Yoni. "Meged Field May Be a (Black) Gold Mine for Israel." *Arutz Sheva* (November 29, 2010). http://www.israelnationalnews.com/News/News.aspx/140899.

Kraemer, Susan. "Israel's Leviathan Gas Find Will Have Widespread Repercussions for World Power." *Green Prophet* (December 31,2010). http://www.greenprophet.com/2010/12/leviathan-gas-israel-balance-of-power/.

Morris, Charles. *The Two Trillion Dollar Meltdown: Easy Money, High Rollers, and the Great Credit Crash.* New York: PublicAffairs, 2008.

Mozgovaya, Natasha and Ravid, Barak. "PM heads to U.S. under threat of Palestinian statehood declaration." *Haaretz.com* (November 8, 2009). http://www.haaretz.com/print-edition/news/pm-heads-to-u-s-under-threat-of-palestinian-statehood-declaration-1.4599.

Netanyahu, Benjamin. "Address by PM Netanyahu to the European Friends of Israel Conference," Israeli Ministry of Foreign Affairs website (February 7, 2011). http://www.mfa.gov.il/MFA/Government/Speeches+by+Israeli+leaders/2011/PM_Netanyahu_European_Friends_Israel_7-Feb-2011.htm.

Obama, Barak. "Speech in Cairo." *New York Times* (June 4, 2009). http://www.nytimes.com/2009/06/04/us/politics/04obama.text.html?pagewanted=all.

Oberman, Mira. "2011 is deadliest US tornado season in 75 years." *AFP* (June 2, 2011), http://www.google.com/hostednews/afp/article/ALeqM5ghhRNeYD7ilot5_4H8Swycjsgw6Q?docId=CNG.c65e713266ca1fce157fea8c232aaa1b.121.

O'Donnell, Lawrence. "The Last Word with Lawrence O'Donnell." Video on MSNBC.com (March 17, 2011). http://www.msnbc.msn.com/id/21134540/vp/42141858#42141858.

Paul, Ron. *End the Fed.* New York: Grand Central Publishing, 2009.

Rosenberg, Joel. *Epicenter 2.0: Why the Current Rumblings in the Middle East Will Change Your Future.* Carol Springs, IL: Tyndale House Publishers, Inc., 2006, 2008.

Saada, Tass. "Finding True Peace in the Middle East: Why Muslims Are Turning to Faith in Jesus Christ and Choosing to Love Israel." *Epicenter Conference 2011* (May 16, 2011). A Panel Discussion with Joel Rosenberg, streaming video, http://www.epicenterconference.com/.

Sada, George. *Saddam's Secrets: How an Iraqi General Defied and Survived Saddam Hussein.* Brentwood, TN: Integrity Publishers, 2006.

Saleh, Heba and England, Andrew. "Gaddafi vows fight to the death." *Financial Times* (February 23, 2011).

Schieffer, Bob. *Face the Nation,* video, March 16, 2011. http://www.cbsnews.com/video/watch/?id=7360900n&tag=related;photovideo.

Sharlat, Hormoz. "Finding True Peace in the Middle East: Why Muslims Are Turning to Faith in Jesus Christ and Choosing to Love Israel." *Epicenter Conference 2011* (May 16, 2011). A Panel Discussion with Joel Rosenberg, streaming video, http://www.epicenterconference.com/.

Smith, James E. *The Major Prophets.* Joplin, MO: College Press Publishing Company, 1995.

Smith, Yves. *Econnned: How Unenlightened Self-interested Undermined Democracy and Corrupted Capitalism.* New York: Palgrave Macmillan, 2010.

Stakelbeck, Erick. "Iranian Video Says Mahdi is 'Near.'" CBN News Website (March 28, 2011). http://www.cbn.com/cbnnews/world/2011/March/Iranian-Regime-Video-Says-Mahdi-is-Near-/.

Toameh, Khaled Abu. "Abbas: No historic compromise on Jerusalem borders." *Jerusalem Post* (September 7, 2010). http://www.jpost.com/MiddleEast/Article.aspx?id=187417.

Uris, Jill and Leon. *Jerusalem, Song of Songs.* New York: Doubleday, 1981.

Voltaire. *The Philosophical Dictionary.* Kindle edition, downloadable at http://www.gutenberg.org/ebooks/18569.

Walsh, Elsa. "The Prince." *The New Yorker* (March 24, 2003).

Webb, Merryn Somerset. "Lessons from Weimar." *MoneyWeek* (August 20, 2010). http://www.moneyweek.com/news-and-charts/economics/merryn-somerset-webb-lessons-from-weimar-50001.

ENDNOTES

1   "US, Israel Will Soon Exit the Middle East: Ahmadinejad," *France 24* (February 11, 2011), http://www.france24.com/en/20110211-us-israel-will-soon-exit-middle-east-ahmadinejad.

2   Ibid.

3   Aleks Tapinsh, "Ahmadinejad joins China, Russia leaders at summit," *Agence France-Press* (AFP News Agency), (June 15, 2011), http://www.google.com/hostednews/afp/article/ALeqM5iK-uoG7aI7dCBPyVCPotpZeFc4Sg?docId=CNG.d8b17504535e4f19218999090de182f4.641.

4   Farhad Pouladi, "Ahmadinejad insists Iran not seeking nuclear bomb," *Agence France-Press* (AFP News Agency), (June 23, 2011), http://www.google.com/hostednews/afp/article/ALeqM5hH8mB4iW9MJ6ElbozG5o8-QlZDqA?docId=CNG.34a096065d43eb06d18ea86500b8f1a9.01.

5   *The Coming Is Upon Us*, streaming video, "Iran Leaders: The Coming is Upon Us – Israel Shall be Destroyed! (Watch the Video)" A Time to Betray website (March 28, 2011), http://atimetobetray.com/blog/iran-leaders-the-coming-is-upon-us—israel-shall-be-destroyed-watch-the-video/.

6   James E. Smith, *The Major Prophets,* Daniel 9:24-27 (Joplin, MO: College Press Publishing Company, 1995).

7   For more on the mystery of the Church, see Ephesians 3:1-12.

8   The Greek word for Church, *ekklesia,* means "called out ones."

9   Several websites mark this book as being released in 1894 or 1895, but according to Google Books the earliest edition was published in 1882, http://books.google.com/books?id=_mLVQAAACAAJ&dq=the+coming+prince:&hl=en&ei=6uI4TaKsNcWXOubX8IEL&sa=X&oi=book_result&ct=result&resnum=3&sqi=2&ved=0CC8Q6AEwAg.

10 Robert Anderson, *The Coming Prince,* http://philologos.org/__eb-tcp/preface.htm.

11 George Bush (1796-1859), *The Valley of Vision; or The Dry Bones of Israel Revived: An Attempted Proof (From Ezekiel, Chapter 37:1-14) of the Restoration and Conversion of the Jews* (New York: Saxton & Miles, 1844), ii-iii.

12 Ibid., iv.

13 Ibid., 21.

14 Ibid., 39.

15 William E. Blackstone, *Jesus Is Coming: God's Hope for a Restless World* (Grand Rapids, MI: Kregel Classics, 1989), 167.

16 For example, see Tom Brokaw's book, *The Greatest Generation.*

17 David B. Barrett and Todd M. Johnson, "Annual Statistical Table on Global Mission: 2004," *International Bulletin of Missionary Research,* Vol. 28, No. 1 (January 2004), 24-25.

18 David B. Barrett and Todd M. Johnson, "Christianity 2011: Martyrs and the Resurgence of Religion," *International Bulletin of Missionary Research* (January 2011), 28-29.

19 Catherine Brahic, "The megaquake connection: Are huge earthquakes linked?" *New Scientist* (March 16, 2011), http://www.newscientist.com/article/mg20928043.000-the-megaquake-connection-are-huge-earthquakes-linked.html.

20 Lawrence O'Donnell, "The Last Word with Lawrence O'Donnell," Video on MSNBC.com (March 17, 2011), http://www.msnbc.msn.com/id/21134540/vp/42141858#42141858.

21 Seth Borenstein and Julie Reed Bell, "2010 Extreme Weather: Deadliest Year in a Generation," *The Huffington Post* (December 22, 2010), http://www.huffingtonpost.com/2010/12/20/2010-extreme-weather-dead_n_798956.html.

22 Mira Oberman, "2011 is deadliest US tornado season in 75 years," *AFP* (June 2, 2011), http://www.google.com/hostednews/afp/article/ALeqM5ghhRNeYD7ilot5_4H8Swycjsgw6Q?docId=CNG.c65e713266ca1fce157fea8c232aaa1b.121.

23 Bob Schieffer on *Face the Nation*, video, March 16, 2011, http://www.cbsnews.com/video/watch/?id=7360900n&tag=related;photovideo.

24 David B. Barrett and Todd M. Johnson, *World Christian Trends AD 30–AD 2200: Interpreting the Annual Christian Megacensus* (Pasadena, CA: William Carey Library, 2001), 229.

25 Barrett and Johnson, "Christianity 2011: Martyrs and the Resurgence of Religion." PAGE NUMBERS?

26   Orla Guerin, "Fear for Pakistan's Death Row Christian Woman," *BBC News* (December 5, 2010), http://www.bbc.co.uk/news/world-south-asia-11923701.

27   Guerin, "Fear for Pakistan's Death Row Christian Woman," *BBC News*.

28   "Murder of Governor in Pakistan Darkens 'Blasphemy' Case," *Compass Direct News* (January 5, 2011), http://www.compassdirect.org/english/country/pakistan/30961/.

29   "Human Rights First Condemns Passage of U.N. Resolution 'Combating Defamation of Religions,'" Human Rights *First* press release (December 21, 2010), http://www.humanrightsfirst.org/2010/12/21/human-rights-first-condemns-passage-of-u-n-resolution-"combating-defamation-of-religions"/.

30   Draft of the "Combating Defamation of Religion," available at http://www.eyeontheun.org/developments-item.asp?d=9299&rid=12464 (Accessed: February 18, 2011).

31   "Right to Believe," Open Doors UK website, http://www.opendoorsuk.org/campaign/RTB.php (Accessed: February 18, 2011).

32   Barrett and Johnson, "Christianity 2011: Martyrs and the Resurgence of Religion." PAGE NUMBERS?

33   "Six Megathemes Emerge from Barna Group Research in 2010," Barna Group Research (December 13, 2010), http://www.barna.org/culture-articles/462-six-megathemes-emerge-from-2010.

34   "Bill Hybels and Bono 1," YouTube (April 10, 2008), http://www.youtube.com/watch?v=grBByc7t3Fs.

35   Audra Jennings, "The Breakthrough of Christianity in the Middle East: Q & A with Tom Doyle, Author of *Breakthrough*," Christian Post Blogs (March 27, 2009), http://blogs.christianpost.com/books/2009/03/the-breakthrough-of-christianity-in-the-middle-east-27/.

36   Joel Rosenberg, *Epicenter 2.0: Why the Current Rumblings in the Middle East Will Change Your Future* (Carol Springs, IL: Tyndale House Publishers, Inc., 2006, 2008), 211.

37   Hormoz Sharlat, "Finding True Peace in the Middle East: Why Muslims Are Turning to Faith in Jesus Christ and Choosing to Love Israel," *Epicenter Conference 2011* (May 16, 2011), A Panel Discussion with Joel Rosenberg, streaming video, http://www.epicenterconference.com/.

38   Rosenberg, *Epicenter 2.0*, 216. NOTE: It is well worth getting a copy of this book to read Mr. Rosenberg's research and other interviews pertaining to this growing phenomenon.

39   Ray Bentley, "Drawing Lessons from the Book of Joel for Israel, the Church, and the Nations," Epicenter Conference 2011 (May 15, 2011), A panel discussion moderated by Joel Rosenberg, streaming video, http://www.epicenterconference.com/.

40   Tass Saada, "Finding True Peace in the Middle East: Why Muslims Are Turning to Faith in Jesus Christ and Choosing to Love Israel," *Epicenter Conference 2011* (May 16, 2011), A Panel Discussion with Joel Rosenberg, streaming video, http://www.epicenterconference.com/.

41   Ray Bentley, "Joel 2:1-17: A Trumpet Call for Israel and the Church," *Epicenter Conference 2011* (May 15, 2011), streaming video, http://www.epicenterconference.com/.

42   Troy Anderson, "A Jewish Awakening?" *Charisma* magazine website (December 9, 2010), http://www.charismamag.com/index.php/newsletters/standing-with-israel/29723-a-jewish-awakening-.

43   Ibid.

44   Barrett and Johnson, "Christianity 2011: Martyrs and the Resurgence of Religion." PAGE NUMBERS?

45   Barrett and Johnson, *World Christian Trends*, 244.

46   Benjamin Netanyahu, "Address by PM Netanyahu to the European Friends of Israel Conference," Israeli Ministry of Foreign Affairs website (February 7, 2011), http://www.mfa.gov.il/MFA/Government/Speeches+by+Israeli+leaders/2011/PM_Netanyahu_European_Friends_Israel_7-Feb-2011.htm.

47   Jessica Guynn, "Google exec Wael Ghonim in Egypt says long live the revolution 2.0." *Los Angeles Times* website (February 11, 2011), http://latimesblogs.latimes.com/technology/2011/02/google-exec-wael-ghonim-in-egypt-says-long-live-the-revolution-20.html.

48   Heba Saleh and Andrew England, "Gaddafi vows fight to the death," *Financial Times* (February 23, 2011), 1.

49   "US, Israel Will Soon Exit the Middle East: Ahmadinejad," *France 24* (February 11, 2011), http://www.france24.com/en/20110211-us-israel-will-soon-exit-middle-east-ahmadinejad.

50   Ibid.

51   "Report: Egypt has approved Iran warships to use Suez Canal," *Haaretz.com* (February 18, 2011), http://www.haaretz.com/news/international/report-egypt-has-approved-iran-warships-to-use-suez-canal-1.344310.

52   "Islamic Mobs Burn Down Church in Egypt," *Compass Direct* (March 8, 2011), http://www.compassdirect.org/english/country/egypt/69546/.

53   Evan Kohlmann, Al-Qaida's Jihad in Europe: The Afghan-Bosnian Network (New York: Berg, 2004), p. 183.

54   Douglas Schoen, *Fox News*, "Why the Muslim Brotherhood Will Win," *Fox News.com* (February 10, 2011), http://www.foxnews.com/opinion/2011/02/10/muslim-brotherhood-win/.

55   Associated Press, "Poll: Over Half of Egypt Wants End to Israel Peace," *NewsMax.com* (April 25, 2011), http://www.newsmax.com/Newsfront/ML-Egypt-Poll/2011/04/25/id/394043.

56   While some have interpreted *Rosh* as being sort of shorthand for "Russia," this seems unlikely since Russia would not have been a land with which Ezekiel was familiar. Since, according to *Strong's Lexicon*, the word *Rosh* means "head" or "chief," some translations such as the ESV have this as "*Gog, of the land of Magog, the chief prince of Meshech and Tubal*." Most, however, use the title "*prince of Rosh, Meshech and Tubal*," echoing the titles given to demonic spirits in Daniel. However, within this, it is uncertain what *Rosh* signifies. Several scholars have suggested it refers to the Assyrian *Rašu*, which was on the northwest border of Elam in Media.

57   Voltaire, *The Philosophical Dictionary*, Kindle edition, downloadable at http://www.gutenberg.org/ebooks/18569, location 1,030.

58   In fact, if you search for "Persepolis" in Google Earth, it will take you to the site of this celebration. In the satellite image, you can still see the five-pointed star of roadways for the pavilions built for the guests of this event.

59   See my book, *The Final Move Beyond Iraq*, for more on this.

60   For more on "Fumbling Iran," see the chapter with that title in my book, *The Final Move Beyond Iraq*.

61   For a quick study of this history, you can get a cursory understanding from the 1966 film *Khartoum*, or one of the various remakes of the film, like *The Four Feathers*, that use the rise of Sudan's Mahdi as a backdrop.

62   Hillary Leila Krieger, "Turkey has embraced the leaders of Iran and HAMAS," *The Jerusalem Post*, June 6, 2011; http://www.jpost.com/International/Article.aspx?id=177577. Accessed July 14, 2011.

63   In the *King James Bible*, this phrase is translated as "*the merchants of Tarshish, with all the young lions thereof*," which throws a different light on the passage, though no clearer. Some suggest again that "*the young lions*" refer to the colonies of Europe [BRITAIN - BECAUSE ITS EMBLEM WAS THE LION?], or perhaps a military group such as NATO.

64   The Shia and Sunni Hadiths differ in content, which is largely why the prophecies of the Twelfth Imam are Shia and not Sunni beliefs—nor do all Shia interpret these scriptures as the leaders of the current Iranian regime do.

65   *The Coming Is Upon Us*, streaming video, "Iran Leaders: The Coming is Upon Us – Israel Shall be Destroyed! (Watch the Video)" A Time to Betray website (March 28, 2011), http://atimetobetray.com/blog/iran-leaders-the-coming-is-upon-us—israel-shall-be-destroyed-watch-the-video/.

66   Erick Stakelbeck, "Iranian Video Says Mahdi is 'Near'," *CBN News* Website (March 28, 2011), http://www.cbn.com/cbnnews/world/2011/March/Iranian-Regime-Video-Says-Mahdi-is-Near-/.

67   *The Coming Is Upon Us*, video.

68   Ibid.

69   Reza Kahlil, interview with Joel Rosenberg presented during "Assessing the Threat of Radical Islam in the Epicenter," streaming video, Epicenter Conference 2011 (May 16, 2011), http://www.epicenterconference.com/.

70   Rosenberg, *Epicenter 2.0*, 333-334.

71   Adrienne S. Gaines, "Company Claims 1.5 Billion Barrels of Oil Found in Israel," *Charisma News* online (August 19, 2010), http://www.charismamag.com/index.php/news/29124-company-claims-15-billion-barrels-of-oil-found-in-israel.

72   Lev & Yoni Kempinski, "Meged Field May Be a (Black) Gold Mine for Israel," *Arutz Sheva* (November 29, 2010), http://www.israelnationalnews.com/News/News.aspx/140899.

73   Gaines, "Company Claims 1.5 Billion Barrels of Oil Found in Israel."

74   Ethan Bronner, "Gas Field Confirmed Off Coast of Israel," *The New York Times* (December 30, 2010), http://www.nytimes.com/2010/12/31/world/middleeast/31leviathan.html?_r=2.

75   Susan Kraemer, "Israel's Leviathan Gas Find Will Have Widespread Repercussions for World Power," *Green Prophet* (December 31,2010), http://www.greenprophet.com/2010/12/leviathan-gas-israel-balance-of-power/.

76   Ibid.

77   "Yom Kippur War: Sacrificial Stand in the Golan Heights," *HistoryNet.com* (June 12, 2006), http://www.historynet.com/yom-kippur-war-sacrificial-stand-in-the-golan-heights.htm/1.

78   Transcription of telephone conversation with Ambassador Michael Oren from Mike Evans' personal files, September 3, 2010.

79   While I have made this assertion before in some of my other books, details of this transfer are outlined in George
     Sada's *Saddam's Secrets: How an Iraqi General Defied and Survived Saddam Hussein* (Brentwood, TN: Integrity
     Publishers, 2006), 258-263.

80   *The Treasury of Scripture Knowledge: Five Hundred Thousand Scripture References and Parallel Passages*,
     Ezekiel 39:11 (Oak Harbor, WA: Logos Research Systems, Inc., 1995).

81   Ambrose Evans-Pritchard, "The Death of Paper Money," *The Telegraph* (July 25, 2010), http://www.telegraph.
     co.uk/finance/comment/ambroseevans_pritchard/7909432/The-Death-of-Paper-Money.html.

82   Merryn Somerset Webb, "Lessons from Weimar," *MoneyWeek* (August 20, 2010), http://www.moneyweek.com/
     news-and-charts/economics/merryn-somerset-webb-lessons-from-weimar-50001.

83   It is worth noting that the United States never signed the Treaty of Versailles for a number of reasons, one of
     which—though probably not the most prominent—was it didn't agree with the excessive price tag levied on
     Germany to reimburse other countries of their costs in the war.

84   Adam Fergusson, *When Money Dies: The Nightmare of Deficit Spending, Devaluation, and Hyperinflation in
     Weimar Germany* (New York: PublicAffairs, 1975), xii.

85   Ibid.

86   *This American Life*, "423: The Invention of Money," *National Public Radio* (January 7, 2011), audio, available at:
     http://www.thisamericanlife.org/radio-archives/episode/423/the-invention-of-money.

87   Ron Paul, *End the Fed* (New York: Grand Central Publishing, 2009), 8-10.

88   "Social Security Benefit Amounts," Social Security online (last updated: October 29, 2010), http://www.ssa.gov/
     oact/cola/Benefits.html.

89   "Investment Banking Jobs—Vice Presidents or Directors," *Trades and Tombstones* website (2009), http://
     investmentbanking.jobsearchdigest.com/97/investment-banking-jobs-vice-president-or-director/.

90   Elsa Walsh, "The Prince," *The New Yorker* (March 24, 2003), 48.

91   Danny Ayalon, interview with Joel Rosenberg during "Assessing the Threat of Radical Islam in the Epicenter,"
     streaming video, Epicenter Conference 2011 (May 16, 2011), http://www.epicenterconference.com/.

92   "Obama promises king Israel will withdraw from West Bank, Jerusalem." Geostrategy-Direct.com (July 7, 2010),
     http://www.geostrategy-direct.com/geostrategy-direct/. (Accessed July 2010).

93   Barak Obama, "Speech in Cairo," *The New York Times* (June 4, 2009), http://www.nytimes.com/2009/06/04/us/
     politics/04obama.text.html?pagewanted=all.

94   Available at http://www.un.int/wcm/webdav/site/palestine/shared/documents/Ending%20Occupation%20
     Establishing%20the%20State%20(August%202009).pdf.

95   Natasha Mozgovaya and Barak Ravid, "PM heads to U.S. under threat of Palestinian statehood
     declaration," *Haaretz.com* (November 8, 2009), http://www.haaretz.com/print-edition/news/
     pm-heads-to-u-s-under-threat-of-palestinian-statehood-declaration-1.4599.

96   Associated Press, "New Round of Mideast Peace Talks Begin," *Las Vegas Sun* (September 9, 2010), http://www.
     google.com/search?sourceid=navclient&ie=UTF-8&rlz=1T4GGLL_enUS382US382&q=l+see+in+you+a+partner
     +for+peace.

97   Khaled Abu Toameh, "Abbas: No historic compromise on Jerusalem borders." *Jerusalem Post* (September 7,
     2010), http://www.jpost.com/MiddleEast/Article.aspx?id=187417.

98   Helene Cooper, "Obama and Netanyahu, Distrustful Allies, Meet," *The New York Times* (May
     19, 2011), http://www.nytimes.com/2011/05/20/world/middleeast/20policy.html?_r=2&WT.
     mc_id=NYT-E-I-NYT-E-AT-0525-L17&pagewanted=all.

99   Benjamin Netanyahu, "Speech by PM Netanyahu to a Joint Meeting of the U.S. Congress," *Israel Ministry of
     Foreign Affairs* website (May 24, 2011), http://www.mfa.gov.il/MFA/Government/Speeches+by+Israeli+leade
     rs/2011/Speech_PM_Netanyahu_US_Congress_24-May-2011.htm.

100 Jill and Leon Uris, *Jerusalem, Song of Songs* (New York: Doubleday, 1981), 9.

101 For more on the discussion of where the United States is in the end times—and specifically in the book of
     Revelation—see my book, *The American Prophecies*.

102 For more on Jerusalem, check out my book, *Cursed: The Conspiracy to Divide Jerusalem* (Phoenix:
     TimeWorthy Books, 2010).

ACKNOWLEDGEMENTS

My sincere appreciation to those people whose hard work and dedication made this book possible: Rick Killian, Peter Gloege, Terry Musclow and the fine folks at Dickinson Press, Elizabeth Sherman, and Arlen and Lanelle (Shaw) Young. It is impossible to write and produce a book without the assistance of a host of people. One of the most important is my beloved wife, Carolyn. Thank you for your patience, compassion, encouragement and sacrifice.